A JOURNEY OF RICHES

Living into Self-Esteem

Collective Wisdom for an
Empowered Self

Published by Motion Media International

Editors: Eric Wyman, Yasmin Phillip, Parker Hansen, Rosemary Lawton, and Arynne Priest

Cover Design: Motion Media International
Typesetting & Assembly: Motion Media International

Printing: Amazon and Ingram Sparks
Creator: John Spender, Primary Author
Title: *A Journey of Riches – Living into Self-Esteem*

ISBN Digital: 978-1-925919-90-5
ISBN Print: 978-1-925919-91-2

Subjects: Motivation, Inspiration, Memoir

ACKNOWLEDGMENTS

⎯⎯⎯⎯⎯⎯⎯⎯⎯⎯⎯⎯⎯⎯⎯⎯⎯

R eading and writing are gifts that very few give to themselves. It is such a powerful way to reflect and gain closure from the past; reading and writing are therapeutic processes. The experience raises one's self-esteem, confidence, and awareness of self.

I learned this when I collated the first book in the *A Journey of Riches* series, which now includes forty books with over 400 co-authors from over 50 countries. Writing about your personal experiences is difficult, and I honor and respect every author who has collaborated in the series.

For many authors, English is their second language, which is a significant achievement. In creating this anthology of short stories, I have been touched by the generosity, gratitude, and shared energy this experience has given everyone.

The inspiration for *Living into Self-Esteem* was born from my desire to share uplifting stories that awaken the sense of worth and self-respect within each of us. Each chapter is written by a different author, offering their unique insights into the transformative journey of embracing one's value, building resilience, and stepping into self-acceptance.

The contributors explore various dimensions of personal growth, from confronting self-doubt and healing old wounds to recognizing inner worth and turning challenges into catalysts for change. Through their reflections and lived experiences, this book invites you on a journey of deep self-discovery and empowerment.

Acknowledgments

Together, these voices remind us that self-esteem is not a fixed state, but a continuous, evolving process, one nourished by courage, self-awareness, and a commitment to honoring who we are. *Living into Self-Esteem* shows that true self-worth is not something we chase, but something we live into, day by day, step by step.

I want to thank all the authors for entrusting me with their unique memories, encounters, and wisdom. Thank you for sharing and opening the door to your soul so others may learn from your experience. I trust the readers will gain confidence from your successes and wisdom from your failures.

I also want to thank my family. I know you are proud of me, seeing how far I have come from that ten-year-old boy learning to read and write at a basic level. So, big shout-out to Mom, Robert, Dad, and Merril; my brother Adam and his daughter Krystal; my sister Hollie and her partner Brian; my nephew, Charlie, and niece, Heidi; thank you for your support. Also to my grandparents, Gran and Pop, and Ma and Pa, who now rest in peace. They accepted me just as I am with all my travels and adventures worldwide.

Thanks to the team at Motion Media International; you have done an excellent job editing and collating this book. It was a pleasure working with you on this successful project, and I thank you for your patience in dealing with the changes and adjustments along the way.

Thank you, the reader, for having the courage to examine your life and consider how you can improve your future in a rapidly changing world.

Again, thank you to my co-authors: **Piera Maria Fromm, Lisa Duckworth, Manuela Lipp, Leigh Huxley, Kandi Roemhildt, Magali Dorffner, Julie Blouin, Liz Pembroke, Kia Stewart, Mat Bankes, Phil Barlow, Rebecca Sarr, and Matthew White**

With gratitude,
John R. Spender

TABLE OF CONTENTS

Table Of Contents

Praise for *A Journey of Riches* Book Series

—————⊸o〰o⊷—————

"The *A Journey of Riches* book series is a great collection of inspiring short stories that will leave you wanting more!"
~ Alex Hoffmann, Network Marketing Guru

"If you are looking for an inspiring read to get you through any change, this is it! This book comprises many gripping perspectives from a collection of successful international authors with a tone of wisdom to share."
~ Theera Phetmalaigul, Entrepreneur/Investor

"*A Journey of Riches* is an empowering series that implements two simple words for overcoming life's struggles.
"By diving into the meaning of the words 'problem' and 'challenge,' you will be motivated to believe in the triumph of perseverance.

With many different authors from all around the world coming together to share various stories of life's trials, you will find yourself drenched in encouragement to push through even the darkest of battles. The stories are heartfelt personal shares of moving through and transforming challenges into rich life experiences.

"The book will move, touch, and inspire your spirit to face and overcome life's adversities. It is a truly inspirational read. Thank you for being the kind, open soul you are, John!"
~ Casey Plouffe, Seven-Figure Network Marketer

"A must-read for anyone facing major changes or challenges in life right now. This book will give you the courage to overcome any struggle with confidence, grace, and ease."
~ Jo-Anne Irwin, Transformational Coach and Best-Selling Author

"I have enjoyed the *A Journey of Riches* book series. Each person's story is written from the heart, and everyone's journey is different. However, we all have a story to tell, and John Spender does an amazing job of finding authors and combining their stories into uplifting books."
~ Liz Misner Palmer, Foreign Service Officer

"A timely read as I'm facing a few challenges right now. I like the various insights from the different authors. This book will inspire you to move through any challenge or change you are experiencing."
~ David Ostrand, Business Owner

"I've known John Spender for a while now, and I was blessed with an opportunity to be in book four in the series. I know that you will enjoy this new journey, like the rest of the books in the series. The collection of stories will assist you with making changes, dealing with challenges, and seeing that transformation is possible for your life."
~ Charlie O'Shea, Entrepreneur

"The *A Journey of Riches* series will draw you in and help you dig deep into your soul. These authors have unbelievable life stories of purpose inside of them. John Spender is dedicated to bringing peace, love, and adventure to the world of his readers! Dive into this series, and you will be transformed!"
~ Jeana Matichak, Author of *Finding Peace*

"Awesome! Truly inspirational! It is amazing what the human spirit can achieve and overcome! Highly recommended!"
~ Fabrice Beliard, Australian Business Coach and Best-Selling Author

"The *A Journey of Riches* series is a must-read. It is an empowering collection of inspirational and moving stories full of courage, strength, and heart. Bringing peace and awareness to those lucky enough to read to assist and inspire them on their life journey."
~ Gemma Castiglia, Avalon Healing, Best-Selling Author

"The *A Journey of Riches* book series is an inspirational collection of books that will empower you to take on any challenge or change in life."
~ Kay Newton, Midlife Stress Buster and Best-Selling Author

"The *A Journey of Riches* book series is an inspiring collection of stories, sharing many different ideas and perspectives on how to overcome challenges, deal with change, and make empowering choices in your life. Open the book anywhere and let your mood choose where you need to read. Buy one of the books today; you'll be glad that you did!"
~ Trish Rock, Modern Day Intuitive, Best-Selling Author, Speaker, Psychic, and Holistic Coach

"*A Journey of Riches* is another inspiring read. The authors are from all over the world, and each has a unique perspective to share that will have you thinking differently about your current circumstances in life. An insightful read!"
~ Alexandria Calamel, Success Coach and Best-Selling Author

"The *A Journey of Riches* book series is a collection of real-life stories, which are truly inspiring and give you the confidence that no matter what you are dealing with in your life, there is a light at the end of the tunnel and a very bright one at that. Totally empowering!"
~ John Abbott, Freedom Entrepreneur

"An amazing collection of true stories from individuals who have overcome great changes and who have transformed their lives and used their experience to uplift, inspire, and support others."
~ Carol Williams, Author, Speaker, and Coach

"You can empower yourself from the power within this book that can help awaken the sleeping giant within you. John has a purpose in life to bring inspiring people together to share their wisdom for the benefit of all who venture deep into this book series. If you are looking for inspiration to be someone special, this book can be your guide."
~ Bill Bilwani, Renowned Melbourne Restaurateur

"In the *A Journey of Riches* series, you will catch the impulse to step up, reconsider, and settle for only the very best for yourself and those around you. Penned from the heart and with an unflinching drive to make a difference for the good of all, the *A Journey of Riches* series is a must-read."
~ Steve Coleman, author of *Decisions, Decisions! How to Make the Right One Every Time*

"Do you want to be on top of your game? *A Journey of Riches* is a must-read with breakthrough insights that will help you do just that!"
~ Christopher Chen, Entrepreneur

"In *A Journey of Riches*, you will find the insight, resources, and tools you need to transform your life. By reading the author's stories, you, too, can be inspired to achieve your greatest accomplishments and what is truly possible for you. Reading this book activates your true potential for transforming your life way beyond what you think is possible. Read it and learn how you, too, can have a magical life."
~ Elaine Mc Guinness, Best Selling Author of *Unleash Your Authentic Self!*

"If you are looking for an inspiring read, look no further than the *A Journey of Riches* book series. The books are an inspiring collection of short stories that will encourage you to embrace life even more. I highly recommend you read one of the books today!"
~ Kara Dono, Doula, Healer, and Best-Selling Author

"The *A Journey of Riches* book series is filled with real-life short stories of heartfelt tribulations turned into uplifting self-transformation by the power of the human spirit to overcome adversity. The journeys captured in these books will encourage you to embrace life in a whole new way. I highly recommend reading this inspiring anthology series."
~ Chris Drabenstott, Best-Selling Author and Editor

"There is so much motivational power in the *A Journey of Riches* series!! Each book is a compilation of inspiring, real-life stories by several different authors, which makes the journey feel more relatable and success more attainable. If you are looking for something to move you forward, you'll find it in one (or all) of these books."
~ Cary MacArthur, Personal Empowerment Coach

"I've been fortunate to write with John Spender, and now, I call him a friend. The *A Journey of Riches* book series features real stories that have inspired me and will inspire you. John has a passion for finding amazing people from all over the world, giving the series a global perspective on relevant subject matters."
~ Mike Campbell, Fat Guy Diary, LLC

"The *A Journey of Riches* series is the reflection of beautiful souls who have discovered the fire within. Each story takes you inside the truth of what truly matters in life. While reading these stories, my heart space expanded to understand that our most significant contribution in this lifetime is to give and receive love. May you also feel inspired as you read this book."
~ Katie Neubaum, Author of *Transformation Calling*

"*A Journey of Riches* is an inspiring testament that love and gratitude are the secret ingredients to living a happy and fulfilling life. This series is sure to inspire and bless your life in a big way. Truly an inspirational read that is written and created by real people, sharing real-life stories about the power and courage of the human spirit."
~ Jen Valadez, Emotional Intuitive and Best-Selling Author

"If you are looking for an inspirational read, look no further than the *A Journey of Riches* book series. The books are an inspiring and educational collection of short stories from the author's soul that will encourage you to embrace life even more. I've even given them to my clients, too, so that their journeys inspire them in life for wealth, health, and everything else in between. I recommend you make it a priority to read one of the books today!"
~ Goro Gupta, Chief Education Officer, Mortgage Terminator, and Property Mentor

PREFACE

I collated this book by thoughtfully selecting authors from around the world, each one courageously sharing their personal experiences and insights on what it truly means to live into self-esteem. This book brings together a mosaic of voices, offering a rich and honest exploration of how self-esteem is developed, tested, and strengthened through the ebb and flow of life.

Each contributor offers a unique perspective, revealing the many ways self-worth can be discovered, reclaimed, and nurtured. These stories highlight that living into self-esteem is not a linear or universal path, but a deeply personal and evolving journey, shaped by challenges faced, lessons learned, and inner strength uncovered along the way.

Storytelling is how humankind has communicated ideas and passed on learning throughout our civilization. While we have become more sophisticated with technology and life in the modern world is now more convenient, there is still much discontent and dissatisfaction. Many people have also moved away from reading books, missing valuable information that can help them move forward with a positive outlook. Moving toward tasks or dreams that scare us builds self-esteem and helps us grow into better versions of ourselves.

I think it is essential to turn off the television, slow down, read, reflect, and take the time to appreciate everything you have in life. Start with an anthology book, as it offers a cornucopia of viewpoints relating to a particular theme. Here, it's fear and how others have dealt with it. We feel stuck in life or have challenges in a particular area because we see problems through the same lens that created them. With this compendium and all the books in the *A Journey of Riches* series, you have many writing styles and perspectives that will help you think about and see your challenges differently, motivating you to elevate your circumstances.

Anthology books are also great because you can start from any chapter and gain valuable insight or a nugget of wisdom without feeling like you missed something from earlier chapters.

I love reading many personal development books because learning and personal growth are vital. If you're not learning and growing, you're staying the same. Everything in the universe is growing, expanding, and changing. If we are not open to different ideas and ways of thinking and being, then even the most skilled and educated can become closed-minded.

This book series aims to open you up to diverse ways of perceiving your reality. It encourages and gives you many avenues of thinking about the same subject. I hope you feel empowered to make a decision that will best suit you in moving forward with your life. As Albert Einstein said, **"We cannot solve problems with the same level of thinking that created them."** So, with Einstein's words in mind, let your mood pick a chapter, or read from the beginning to the end and be guided to the answers you seek.

With gratitude,
John R. Spender

"You alone are enough. You have nothing to prove to anybody."

— Maya Angelou

Breaking Free from Comparison: Embracing the Power of Self-Esteem

By Julie Blouin

"Our deepest fear is not that we are inadequate.
Our deepest fear is that we are powerful beyond measure.
It is our light, not our darkness that most frightens us.
We ask ourselves, 'Who am I to be brilliant, gorgeous,
talented, fabulous?' Actually, who are you not to be?"
— Marianne Williamson

B reaking free from comparison isn't just about ignoring what others think; it's about owning your confidence and refusing to shrink to fit someone else's expectations. When you truly know who you are and own your strengths, not much can shake you. True self-esteem isn't built on external validation; it's rooted in your ability to stand tall in your own worth, knowing deep in your soul that you are already enough.

I've come to realize that the quiet confidence and inner strength I embody today didn't appear overnight. They are the result of embracing self-esteem, learning to trust myself, and understanding that living authentically is not about proving anything; it's about showing up as enough, no matter the challenges.

Living with self-esteem isn't just about confidence or success; it's about courage. It's about pursuing your goals and dreams with every ounce of determination, no matter how uncomfortable the journey gets. It's about standing tall in the face of doubt and trusting in your worth.

This chapter is deeply personal to me because I've walked the path of self-doubt, battled the discomfort of comparison, and experienced the profound transformation that comes from choosing to believe in myself. I've seen how living with self-esteem reshapes the way we see ourselves, handle setbacks, and show up in the world when others are watching our every move.

I'm writing this chapter because I want to share what I've learned along the way: the lessons, the struggles, and the breakthroughs that made me who I am today. More than anything, I want to share these truths with you. This chapter is an invitation to explore what self-esteem truly means and how it can empower you to live boldly, authentically, and with an unshakable sense of self-worth.

Building self-esteem is the key to unlocking one's full potential

Growing up as an identical twin, I often found myself navigating the delicate balance between individuality and the constant comparisons to my sister. Being a twin is a unique experience, one that few truly understand. My sister and I were always seen together, but beneath the surface, there was so much more to each of us than my mirror reflection.

At times, it felt like my existence was tied to hers—that I was just one half of a whole. My identity often felt blurred in the shadow of "the twins." People rarely saw us as individuals; they saw us as an inseparable pair.

There was comfort in the unity but also a sense of being lost in it. How could I find my voice when our bond was so strongly defined? How could I step out of the shadow of being "half" and show the world who I truly was?

People were always comparing us: who was smarter, funnier, taller, or more outgoing? Who had better grades? Who was more athletic? Who had the better style? Every difference was pointed out. And then came the question we heard on repeat: "You two look exactly alike, but wait, who's the older one again?" No matter who we talked to, the ten-minute gap between our births seemed to fascinate people as if it held some profound significance. It was as if being "the older one" or "the younger one" shaped our identities in the eyes of the world.

The constant comparisons were heavy, sometimes leading to self-doubt. People treated me as though I was in constant competition, as if there could only be one "best twin." Rarely did anyone take the time to call me by my name, afraid they might mix us up. Instead, it was easier to say "the twins." It made me question whether I was enough, whether I would ever be seen for who I truly was, outside of being a twin.

But the truth is, life isn't a race. There's no need to compete when you realize that growth and progress matter more than being "the best." There didn't need to be a winner between us. The goal was simply to show up as the best versions of ourselves, not in competition with each other but in a way that allowed us both to shine and inspire one another.

Being a twin is about more than just looking alike. It's about how rare it is for two people to appear so similar yet be so different. Our bond as twins was often seen as a novelty, something rare and fascinating. And when you're both beautiful, the stares seem to linger a little longer.

I heard the same comments over and over again: "Two of you? That's like a dream come true." It was as if being identical and attractive made us part of some fantasy, something out of a late-night movie. People saw us as an idea, a concept to be admired, an exotic prize to be won or fantasized about. But while our beauty may set us apart, it does not define us.

Our worth isn't in how we look; it's in who we are beneath the surface. It's in our kindness, our individuality, our character, our intelligence, and our strength.

Growing up as twins meant discovering not just who I was in relation to her but who I was outside of that connection. Only when I embraced my individuality did I realize that our bond didn't diminish who I was; it gave me the strength to stand in my own light.

Collaboration became our secret superpower. Instead of seeing each other as rivals, we learned how to lean on each other for support. We learned to complement each other, to bring out the best in one another, and to work as a team. Life isn't about outshining those around you; it's about finding ways to shine together.

The magic of being a twin isn't just about having someone by my side; it's about learning how to thrive together.

The greatest gift of being a twin is realizing that unity and uniqueness can beautifully coexist. It taught me the importance of collaboration over comparison. We are a team, reaching milestones together, navigating challenges side by side, and encouraging each other as we chase our dreams.

This perspective shaped my understanding of self-worth. This journey laid the foundation for how I began to see myself and my value. Through it, I learned powerful lessons about self-esteem: what it truly means to live authentically, embrace individuality, and build unshakable confidence. These lessons became the solid foundation for my life.

Here are five key insights I gained about living with self-esteem that forever shaped my understanding of my own value.

1. Authenticity Is Your Greatest Strength

"Be yourself; everyone else is already taken."
— Oscar Wilde

Your character is built in the moments when no one is watching; when there's no applause or audience. It's easy to wear a mask when others are looking, but true self-esteem is rooted in quiet integrity. Most people live on autopilot, imitating others without ever exploring what truly ignites their soul. But when you embrace your individuality, you begin to master the art of self-esteem.

To do so, you must care less about what others think and more about how you feel. Stop holding yourself back based on people's opinions, and instead, focus on your strengths. Build a foundation of confidence so strong that no external force can shake it. Your worth isn't measured by comparison or by how well you meet others' expectations. Instead, it's shaped by the depth of your character, the integrity of your actions, and the authenticity of your being.

Strip away the superficial: the clothes, the car, the house, the title, the social media following, and the size of your bank account. What's left? Your true self. Your worth is shaped by your choices, the way you treat others, and how you show up in the world. Everything else is just noise, clouding the true reflection of who you are.

Authenticity is the inner compass that guides you, freeing you from the need for external validation. It means standing firm in your identity and being unapologetically yourself. The more authentic you are, the more freedom you experience. Self-esteem doesn't come from pretending to be someone you're not; it's built by embracing who you're meant to be. True confidence is walking into any room knowing you belong simply because you are yourself.

Your individuality sets you apart. You are one-of-a-kind, something that no one else can replicate. Your passions, values, and perspectives are uniquely yours. And the best part? You don't have to meet anyone else's standards to be worthy. Authenticity is the most powerful gift you can give yourself. It's what makes you truly stand out.

2. You Are Enough Just as You Are

> *"Self-worth comes from one thing:*
> *thinking that you are worthy."*
> **— Dr. Wayne Dyer**

You don't need to change, compete, or prove anything to anyone. Who you are is already enough. Self-esteem isn't about meeting others' expectations or checking off society's boxes. It's about knowing deep down that your worth isn't conditional. You are enough. Say it until it becomes a part of you: *I am enough.*

Standing tall in the face of adversity takes courage. Some days, self-doubt will whisper that you're not good enough. But self-esteem silences that voice by proving, through action, that you're capable. Your value isn't tied to accomplishments; it's rooted in your resilience and your willingness to keep showing up, even when life gets tough.

True self-esteem means pursuing your goals without hesitation, fear, or quitting, no matter how many obstacles stand in your way. It means trusting yourself so deeply that you don't need a backup plan out of fear of failure. A person with self-esteem doesn't entertain the idea of defeat. They believe in success, not because they expect everything to go perfectly, but because they know setbacks don't define them. How they rise does. Failure isn't the end; it's a stepping stone. Self-esteem isn't built on guarantees. It's built on faith in yourself and the courage to keep moving forward. Each step reinforces the truth: *I am enough, and I will succeed.*

It's easy to fall into the comparison trap, watching what others are doing, achieving, or flaunting. But those distractions pull you away from your own journey. Your dreams don't exist in someone else's story; they live in yours. Every moment spent comparing yourself to others is time given away instead of invested in your own growth. Tune out the noise. Stop playing the comparison game. Redirect that energy back to yourself and focus on what truly matters.

Your environment also shapes your self-esteem. The media you consume, from TV shows to social media, can subtly influence how you feel about yourself. Advertisements and societal pressures thrive on making you feel inadequate, convincing you that you need something more to be worthy. But that's an illusion. You are already whole, complete, and worthy as you are.

Be mindful of what you allow into your life. Consume content that uplifts and inspires you. Surround yourself with people and experiences that nourish your confidence and encourage your growth. Self-esteem flourishes when you embrace this truth: *I am enough.*

3. Boundaries: Protect Your Self-Worth

"Daring to set boundaries is about having the courage to love ourselves, even when we risk disappointing others."
— Brené Brown

Setting boundaries is a profound act of self-love and self-respect. Boundaries protect what matters most: your self-worth, peace, and dreams. When you set a boundary, you're making a conscious choice to safeguard your long-term goals from being derailed by short-term distractions or fleeting pleasures.

A boundary isn't just a refusal or a wall; it's a doorway to self-respect, allowing in what aligns with your worth and shutting out what doesn't. Saying "no" to distractions means saying "yes" to your bigger vision. Far from being selfish, setting boundaries requires courage. It means prioritizing what truly matters, even when it's uncomfortable. It's choosing purpose over instant gratification, knowing that the fulfillment of your dreams far outweighs the fleeting satisfaction of distractions.

By limiting distractions, resisting unhealthy habits, and delaying gratification, you build discipline. Each time you uphold a boundary, you reinforce your belief in your ability to reach your long-term goals. It's a reminder that short-term pleasure or comfort will never compare to the fulfillment of living a purpose-driven life.

Every time you say "no" to something misaligned with your goals, you're saying "yes" to your future. Boundaries empower you to choose purpose over momentary satisfaction, knowing that staying true to yourself brings far greater rewards.

People who truly value and respect you will support your dreams, not ask you to compromise them. Surround yourself with those who encourage your growth and understand that your journey may require difficult decisions. By focusing on what truly matters, you reinforce your self-worth. You affirm that your goals and dreams are important and that you're willing to work hard to make them a reality. Staying true to your vision requires discipline, perseverance, and self-respect. Boundaries are not barriers; they are bridges to the life you are meant to live.

4. Growth Takes Courage

"Owning our story and loving ourselves through the process is the bravest thing we'll ever do."
— Brené Brown

Pursuing your dreams is not for the faint of heart. It demands effort, determination, and courage. It requires stepping into the unknown, leaving behind the safety of your comfort zone, and daring to do what you've never done before.

True growth requires bravery, the courage to confront the parts of yourself that feel unworthy, to sit with the discomfort of failure, and to push forward despite the voice inside telling you to quit. Building self-esteem isn't about pretending the journey is easy. It's about showing up even when it's hard. It's about leaning into the discomfort of growth and trusting that the struggle is shaping you into someone stronger and more capable. Every obstacle is a chance to rise, to prove to yourself that you are resilient.

Life will test you. There will be moments when your goals feel out of reach, when doubt creeps in, and when giving up seems easier than pushing forward. But determination is built in the moments when you choose to show up, time and time again, not by counting how many times you've fallen, but by rising each time. The strength you gain through these experiences becomes the foundation of your self-worth.

Growth happens when you are stretched, challenged, and tested. So lean into the discomfort with courage, knowing that every challenge is shaping you into the person you are meant to become.

5. Focus on Progress, Not Perfection

*"Personal power means the ability to take action,
to follow through, to take the steps that are necessary
to take an idea and translate it into reality."*
— Tony Robbins

The pursuit of perfection creates unrealistic expectations and can leave you feeling like you're never enough. Perfection is a myth that keeps people stuck in inaction, immobilized by fear. Building self-esteem comes from showing up, especially when life feels uncertain, hard, or messy.

Pain has a way of shaking us to our core. It strips away the illusions we hold on to and forces us to confront our deepest fears: the raw, unfiltered truths. Pain is not the enemy; it is our greatest teacher. It shows us the path to transformation. Progress isn't about avoiding struggle; it's about moving through it, learning from it, and emerging with unshakable self-worth.

When you embrace progress, you stop waiting for the 'perfect' moment to start and begin appreciating the beauty of simply trying. It's about recognizing that every step forward, no matter how small, is a win. It's about being present, persistent, and kind to yourself as you evolve. Progress is where confidence grows, where we learn, adapt, and become stronger.

In the end, the goal isn't perfection; it's continuous growth and transformation. It's about moving forward, learning as you go, and becoming a better version of yourself every day. True fulfillment comes from the journey of self-improvement, not from chasing some unattainable ideal. Progress over perfection is a mindset shift that reminds you that becoming the person you're meant to be happens one step at a time.

Living with self-esteem means embracing the truth that your worth is not defined by the opinions or expectations of others. It's about recognizing that you already have everything you need within yourself to navigate life's challenges and create the reality you desire.

Comparison is a trap that keeps you focused on what others are doing, pulling your attention away from the beauty and growth unfolding within you. When you stop comparing yourself to others, you begin to see your own unique value, and that's where your true power resides.

Self-esteem isn't about being perfect or flawless. It's about showing up for yourself every day with commitment and courage. It's about trusting your own path, even when the world may try to pull you off course.

Kindness doesn't mean you're a people-pleaser. It's about setting boundaries and having the courage to protect your energy. Progress is the focus, not perfection. The critics of the world, those who sit on the sidelines, have no power over you because you are committed to living from a place of self-worth, not external approval.

You are your only competition, and your greatest victory is the relentless pursuit of becoming the best version of yourself.

Your journey is yours alone, and the only way through it is with strength, resilience, and the unshakable belief that you are enough.

Stand tall in your authenticity. Let go of the need for external validation. Be unapologetically you, and know that your worth is written in your character. You don't need to prove it to anyone.

Your self-esteem is the foundation upon which you build your dreams, and when you trust in yourself, there is nothing you cannot achieve.

This is your story. Own it with confidence, live it with courage, and never let comparison dim your light.

All my love, always and forever.

"Owning our story and loving ourselves through that process is the bravest thing that we'll ever do."

— Brené Brown

The Shattered Mirror: A Journey from Psychosis to Self-Esteem

By Mat Bankes

I push myself up from the cold floor, my head pounding. The air is thick with antiseptic, the walls a horrible dull mustard color, while a single window cuts a beam of sunlight into the small, sterile space. It looks like a cell. A hospital maybe? It feels like a nightmare.

A heavy steel door slams shut, bolted from the outside. Through a small glass panel at the top of the door appears a hallway, white and lifeless. Beside me, a flimsy foam mattress, a cardboard cup of water, and a small book with the title *Patient's Rights Handbook* staring up at me like a cruel joke.

Less than an hour ago, I was blissfully relaxing on my front porch, smoking a cigarette while basking in the morning sun, listening to the waves crash against the shore from a distance. But why the hell am I here?

Only moments ago, three security guards forcefully pinned me down, pressing my face into the floor. Multiple hands aggressively ripped my clothes off my body until my bare skin bore down against the cold tiles. Then, a hospital gown was forced upon me, the uniform of the sick, the wounded… the insane.

Surely, this is a mistake. Maybe someone's playing a prank on me. Or perhaps I'm hallucinating? I'm not crazy... Am I?

The room around me seems to send me a clear message. It feels like a scene from a horror film, a haunted asylum filled with lost souls clawing from the depths of their broken minds. But I'm lucid. Cognitive. Aware. Awake. So why is my world reflecting to me one of insanity?

How could I feel so normal on the inside while my external reality is so wildly opposed?

Self-doubt starts to slither inside my mind. How can I figure out what's real? What's true? Is everything I believe about myself, about my experience, wrong?

I soon learned that my self-esteem isn't about how the rest of the world sees me. It's a war between how we see ourselves. The rest of the world simply reflects that back to us.

And right now, my reflection is completely shattered. Reflecting a world of loss, confusion, fear, misidentification, and a completely depleted sense of self-esteem.

How do I get out of here?

The Roots of Low Self-Esteem: Ignorance and Misidentification

Two weeks before my mind and reality shattered and I landed myself in the psych ward, my little coastal town was buzzing with the energy of the annual Jazz Festival. It should have been a weekend of music, good vibes, and kicking back by the beach with friends. But instead, it became something else entirely, something I never saw coming. It marked the beginning of a decade-long journey of escaping the insane reality created within my mind. The journey entailed unraveling false identities and rediscovering true self-esteem.

To mask a superficial sense of self-worth, like so many others before me, I'd spent years chasing stimulation, mistaking it for meaning and satisfaction. Whether it was work, relationships, substances, or distractions, I kept pushing for something more, something to drown out the poor image I held of myself. The feelings of hopelessness, worthlessness, and the sense that I was unloved and only a burden on the ones I loved and society... I wasn't looking for an escape. I was avoiding a confrontation. A confrontation with these demons which resided within the depths of my inner self. They'd plagued me for so long.

I thought I had everything under control that weekend. I'd planned to casually experiment with psychedelics alongside some friends. A small, manageable dose. Just enough to take my mind away from the reality of myself. But control is a slippery slope when you don't really know what's controlling you.

One moment, I was having laughs, guiding my friends through their first psychedelic experience. The next? I was convincing myself I needed a little more. And a little more. And then, well, I ended up having far too much more.

By the time the sun cracked over the horizon, the night had unraveled into something else entirely. I had pushed past the point of return, past the point of reason. A normal trip should have lasted a few hours, where mine was about to stretch longer than a month with no sign of ever stopping. Finally, my mind had won. It had completely set aside the reality it had been fighting and repurposed itself into a different state completely. My body may still be alive, but my mind met its death.

Eventually, I was hurled into the clutches of a psychiatric facility to ensure my safety and that of the public. No longer was I capable of functioning in society. I was now in a space where many people never escape.

Looking back, it's easy to blame drugs for the mental collapse into insanity, but the drugs weren't to blame. They simply pulled back the curtain on something that had been brewing beneath the surface for years. The horrible and self-deprecating view of myself generated through ignorance and misidentification was at a boiling point and required drastic intervention, which the drug-induced psychosis exposed with the breaking of my mind.

I had spent my life to that point dodging the truth. Childhood wounds such as abandonment, control, rejection, shame, and much more had taken control and all combined to harden into a false self-image. This naturally resulted in a superficial self-esteem manufactured to help me survive but never thrive. It required constant validation, constant proof I was worthy and enough. But self-worth built on external approval is about as sturdy as a sandcastle at high tide.

So when the walls came down, they came crashing down hard.

Nevertheless, I ended up locked in a mental ward, staring at the wall, asking myself the one question that kept looping in my mind: How did I get here?

The more I thought about it, the more confusing it became. I thought I was in touch with reality, but if I genuinely was not… then maybe I'd been wrong about everything. This begged the question, what else have I been so wrong about? Everything I thought I knew as fact or truth became a contender for the chopping block to validate its truth. Love, relationships, meaning, existence, everything.

My entire worldview instantly became a fragile house of cards. What was once solid and matter-of-fact became liquid and impermanent like water slipping right through my fingers, incapable of being grasped.

So then, who am I? What am I? What is real? I thought I knew… so what else was I wrong about? It appeared my entire identity was built on avoiding me. So then who the hell am I, really?

Many people try their best to avoid asking themselves these kinds of questions. Like me, it's often much easier to double down on whatever ignorant story we've been telling ourselves for years, rather than face the unknown or uncomfortable truth. But true self-esteem doesn't come from clinging to illusions. After being forced to face myself, and with much support, guidance, mentoring, and self-inquiry, I learned it comes from courageously tearing down our false attachments to misidentifications. And I was only just at the precipice of learning that the hard way.

The Turning Point: A Seed of True Self-Worth

Curiosity burned through me, igniting an unintentional journey into the unknown. If I was ever going to quiet the chaos in my mind and finally find order, truth, and develop genuine self-esteem, I needed to start by identifying my blind spots, and there were plenty.

Then came the barrage of bigger existential questions: Who are we? What are we? What is Truth? What is the meaning of life? What's the point of our existence? The seemingly unanswerable questions kept crashing over me like waves. The answers? Nowhere in sight.

I was at a crossroads, teetering on the edge. One path was familiar: the slow self-destruction of a man lost in his mind. I could see where it led: addiction, regret, and an inevitable, tragic ending. A life where I numbed myself into nothingness, repeating the same cycles, sinking deeper into fear, insecurity, self-loathing, and shame.

The other path? Uncertain. Terrifying. But it was the only one that offered something different: a chance at developing true self-esteem, at reclaiming my identity, at building a life that mattered. It wasn't an easy choice.

The darkness was familiar, the pain predictable. Stepping into my potential meant confronting all the beliefs I had clung to: the ones that told me I wasn't enough, that I was disposable, that I didn't deserve happiness. And that was terrifying.

The devil we know is often more comforting than the one we don't.

Through the thickness of the journey amid the demons I'd strived to slay, I felt like I was fighting an impossible battle. Along this path to recovery, I found myself late one night standing on the shoreline, feet buried in the cold sand, the hum of passing traffic in the distance. The weight of my mistakes, my failures, my impact on others, and the imposing battle that had no light at the end of the tunnel all felt unbearable. A thought crept in: Would the world be better without me?

I don't know if I was truly ready to end my life, but as I stood there, staring into the abyss, I considered the possibility, wondering if I should simply swim into the jaws of the horizon until I was nothing but a distant memory.

Then, at that moment, something surfaced: a story I had read years ago. Buckminster Fuller, a visionary thinker, had once stood at his breaking point. At 32, drowning in failure and despair, he almost ended his life. But at that moment, feeling like he hadn't given 100% to his life as of yet, he made a radical decision: instead of dying right there and then, he would turn his life into an experiment.

He asked himself: what is the maximum advantage I can give to others with the minimum of myself?

Bucky's story hit me like a jolt of electricity. Can I honestly, hand on heart, say that I have given 100% to my life so far? Of course, I couldn't. What if, instead of erasing myself, I maintained my rebuild? What if I committed to something bigger than me? What might be possible?

That night, I made a commitment to myself. I committed to step into the unknown. To face my fears. To challenge the deeply ingrained beliefs that had kept me shackled. To fight the battle despite the lack of light at the end of the tunnel. If needed, I'll fight in the dark for as long as it takes!

And I did... and still do.

It turns out it was less about learning and much more about unlearning.

My mind had been overflowing with assumptions, justifications, excuses, and outdated beliefs. If I was ever going to change, I needed to strip it all down.

So it begins.

I started clearing the debris, including old narratives, toxic thought patterns, and fears disguised as facts. I realized self-esteem isn't something you "get." It's what's left when you remove everything that isn't true about yourself.

The journey from psychosis to kenosis, from being trapped in fear, ego, and self-sabotage to emptying ourselves of falsehood and reconnecting with something real, was just the beginning.

It was time to face the devil I didn't know.

During the initial journey of deconstructing my old ways and beginning to plant new seeds to grow genuine self-esteem, three key pillars kept me grounded and majorly supported the process: vulnerability, self-compassion, and having a healthy balance of an open mind and skepticism.

1. Vulnerability

I had spent years avoiding myself, numbing pain with substances, distractions, and empty validation. But if I wanted to build true self-esteem, I knew I had to start by being brutally honest with myself. It was hard at the start, but I have since learned that vulnerability wasn't weakness; it is actually the most courageous thing to do and the key to breaking free.

Can you embrace vulnerability and identify any areas of discomfort in your life currently? Remember, fear isn't our enemy. Fear is the signpost to our next level of growth toward true self-esteem. Be bold and courageous with your self-inquiry.

2. Self-Compassion

A mentor once told me something that shattered my old ways of thinking. I was having a tough time feeling out of place in the world, uncertain on my path, and down about my lack of passion for life in general. One day after opening up to him, he told me, "Whatever you're doing at this moment, that is your purpose. Own where you are at, accept and have gratitude for the moment and everything it offers, do not focus on what you do not have, and don't make yourself wrong for it."

That hit me. Hard. I had spent my entire life judging myself so harshly, feeling like I was never doing enough. But real self-worth doesn't come from tearing yourself down. It comes from accepting yourself fully, especially in your lowest moments. For me, this is where it all started.

Learning self-compassion wasn't easy, and it didn't happen overnight. It was a practice, and it still is. But the moment we stop seeing ourselves as "less than" and start seeing ourselves as someone in progress, everything shifts. We unlock the learner's mindset.

What area of your life is currently offering you a learning opportunity to show yourself more compassion?

3. An Open Mind with Healthy Skepticism

Trapped in rigid thinking, clinging to beliefs that no longer served me. But letting go didn't mean believing everything blindly; it meant questioning everything with an open mind and healthy skepticism.

Balancing curiosity with discernment was key. If I had shut my mind completely, I would definitely have stayed stuck in the abyss of self-despair, and if I had blindly accepted every new idea, I would have fallen into more dogmatic beliefs and illusions. The sweet spot is staying open but never losing our ability to think critically.

With this balance, I became far more intentional and aware of what sources of information I gained knowledge from and what wisdom I gave the authority to make up my reality.

Think about what beliefs you might hold as true that are purely based on someone else's word. Often, religion, even science, is largely based on beliefs we hold based on things we are told without having our own first-hand experience, essentially outsourcing our truth to others.

Curiosity, vulnerability, and self-compassion cracked something open inside me. For the first time, glimpses of real self-esteem shone through. They were not the kind built on achievements or external validation, but the kind that existed by itself and for itself. Nothing more, nothing less

The work wasn't finished. Not even close. But there was a willingness to start and a commitment to do whatever it takes to keep moving forward.

And that was enough for now.

The Journey of Authentic Self-Esteem: Psychosis to Kenosis

Human development follows a predictable pattern of construction and deconstruction. First, we build our worldview by absorbing beliefs, ideas, and societal expectations. Then, if we're lucky (or forced into it), we deconstruct everything we thought we knew. What's left is the foundation of Truth, the basis of true self-esteem.

As children, we learn how to navigate the world, including relationships, love, money, success, and identity. We assign meaning to everything. Over time, these meanings form the lens through which we see ourselves. But what if that lens is warped? What if the beliefs we built our lives on are faulty? Rarely do people ever take the time to question the integrity of their own mind.

Most people focus on accumulating breadth of knowledge, usually intending to advance their careers to become "experts" in their field. Few dare to explore depth of knowledge, the deeper layers of self-awareness and existence that force us to question everything. Depth requires courage, and for those who seek it, the journey usually begins at rock bottom. At a breaking point.

For me, it took losing my mind

Construction to Deconstruction

After my breakdown, my mind cracked open to questions I had never truly asked before. Things like:

- What if I assume everything I thought I knew was wrong?

- Who am I beyond my achievements, my status, my past, or my pain?

- Is my internal and external reality connected, and if so, how?

- What is Truth?

True Self-esteem isn't built through external validation. It comes from stripping away false narratives until only the truth remains. And that process? It's messy.

As a child, I was abandoned by someone I loved deeply. I made it mean that I was unlovable. Yes, by others, but at a deeper level by me. I didn't love myself. That belief became my inner state, and that inner state became my reality, shaping my decisions, my relationships, and my sense of self-worth. I numbed the pain through self-sabotage, addiction, and distraction. I built an identity around avoidance. But identity is just a story we tell ourselves, and stories can be rewritten.

What is a belief or story you have told yourself about yourself that may not be true and limit you to this day?

The Cleanup: Removing What Doesn't Belong

Rebuilding self-esteem largely involves removing what isn't true. It's a cleanup job.

Everything in our belief system is fair game and must be examined:

- Does this belief empower me or keep me small?

- Is this idea based on fear or love?

- Does this story about myself still serve me?

Bruce Lipton, in *The Biology of Belief*, explains that on a cellular level, we are always in one of two states: contraction (fear) or expansion (love). Every thought, every emotion, and belief falls into one of these categories.

If fear is keeping you stuck, clean it up.

That annoying coworker? Childhood trauma? Financial stress? Every challenge is an opportunity to grow. The external world mirrors what needs attention within us.

What is one belief you can identify to clean up that will have an immediate positive impact on your self-esteem?

From Psychosis to Kenosis: Emptying the False Self

True self-esteem requires letting go of everything that keeps you small, including attachments, fears, and outdated identities.

Is it easy? Hell no! It's painful, confronting, and relentless. Most people avoid this work because it forces them to face parts of themselves they'd rather ignore.

But for those who take the journey? It's worth it.

Through this process, my very sense of identity was questioned:

- What is a person?

- Why do we do what we do, and is there a purpose to it all?

- Where do I end, and the world begins?

- Am I one with, or separate, from everything?

The depth of our questions dictates the depth of our transformation. Ask better questions, get better answers.

If you ask, "Why am I stuck?" your mind will find proof of why you're stuck. If you ask, "How can I break free?" your mind will start looking for solutions.

Your questions create your reality. So ask high-quality questions and avoid low-quality BS.

What is a high-quality question you can start asking yourself today to allow your mind to generate a high-quality answer?

Lessons on Self-Esteem: What Psychosis Taught Me

Losing touch with reality shattered everything I thought I knew. It forced me to question not just the world around me but also myself.

Who was I, really?

Once the illusion of my external reality crumbled, I had no choice but to turn inward. Perhaps that's where real self-esteem begins, not in the outside world, but in the moment we stop outsourcing our worth and start confronting what's within.

So let me ask you: what in your life feels misaligned? What truth have you been avoiding? Because if there's an area where you feel stuck, exhausted, or lost, it might just be the door you need to walk through that will lead to your transformation into ever greater levels of self-esteem.

The Power of "I Don't Know"

I used to believe that "I" was my mind and my body. That my thoughts were Truth. That my emotions defined me. Oh, how times have changed.

Here's something I've learned and hope to pass on: A belief is just another way of saying "I don't know." It's a placeholder we use when we're not yet ready to admit our ignorance. But the moment we embrace "I don't know," that's when real self-inquiry begins and self-awareness is exposed.

Three Levels of Self-Awareness

The (simplified) layers of self-awareness as taught by the Mystic and Yogi Maharishi Mahesh Yogi helped me begin developing a greater perspective of the Self, which I feel is valuable to share:

1. The Cosmic Self: The part of us that exists beyond time and space, whose purpose is experiencing infinite possibilities.

2. The Soul Self: The energetic part of us whose purpose is to grow, expand, and evolve.

3. The Human Self: The part of us that exists in this world, whose purpose is to create and express authentically.

When I saw life through these lenses, something shifted. Instead of feeling like a victim of circumstances, I saw every experience, good or bad, as an opportunity. Either I was winning or I was learning. There was no "losing."

You are a human being riding the waves of the cosmic infinitude of experiences, gifted the opportunity to approach every new experience authentically, and your soul grows and evolves through your ability to learn from every new experience gained. It's a win, win, win.

If you can embrace this perspective and allow yourself to see life this way, the fear fades, because nothing is wasted, nothing is random. Everything, every hardship, every challenge, every perceived failure, is part of something bigger. It's all here to help you step into your fullest and best self.

The Greatest Freedom: Authentic Expression

Here's the thing about self-esteem: It's impossible to build when we're living out of alignment with our truth.

When we silence our authentic selves to fit in, when we play small to avoid conflict, when we suppress our real feelings and opinions, we trade authenticity for approval.

And at what cost? Our self-worth!

The moment I started expressing myself honestly, standing up for what I believed in, challenging my limiting beliefs, and refusing to shrink to make others comfortable, everything changed. Little by little, inch by inch. My confidence grew, not because I suddenly "became" someone different, but because I was finally allowing myself to be who I had always been. Practicing moment to moment. Sometimes I'd do great, and other times I'd fail, but my commitment to continue practicing and never give up was solid.

The Biggest Lie about Self-Esteem

Most people think self-esteem is about building yourself up. But in my experience, it's actually about letting go.

Letting go of:

- False identities we've clung to for validation.

- Fear-based thinking keeping us small.

- The belief that we need external validation to be worthy.

To reiterate, self-esteem isn't something you get. It's something you uncover when you strip away everything that isn't truly you.

What is one thing you can practice letting go of that will have an immediate impact on your self-esteem today?

Your Challenges Are Your Training Ground

So let me ask you, where have you grown the most in life? Was it through ease and success? Or was it through pain, failure, and challenge?

Of course, you know the answer.

Every struggle shapes you. Every challenge forces you to step into something greater.

So next time life throws you into the fire, remember that this is your next growth spurt. This is the moment you get to decide: Will I contract in fear, or will I expand in love?

Choose expansion. Choose You.

And most of all, enjoy the ride, no matter how tough and hopeless it may appear on the surface. If I can dig my way out of the pit of being a mental case in a psych ward, then you can face and conquer whatever challenge life throws at you, too.

A Call to Action: Build Self-Esteem through Self-Realization

If you're searching for true self-esteem, the kind that isn't dependent on success, validation, or circumstances, then your journey begins here.

Another perspective is thinking of self-esteem as a consciousness system, constantly evolving. At its core, it operates in one of two states:

- High entropy (disorder): Fear, ego, selfishness, resistance, and stagnation.

- Low entropy (harmony): Love, courage, awareness, and wisdom.

Everything we think, feel, and do moves us towards one of these states. The key? Recognizing which direction we're heading and creatively choosing differently when needed.

Here are five key areas of practice that I utilize every single day to maintain and continue to develop my true self-esteem:

1. Get a High-Level Perspective on Your Life

Understanding where you are and where you're heading can be life-changing. Frameworks like spiral dynamics, ego development theory, integral theory, and the hero's journey offer powerful insights into your personal growth. They help you see the patterns in your life: what's shaping you, what's limiting you, and what's next.

2. Master Your Breath

What's the simplest, most powerful tool for self-mastery? Your breath.

- The way you breathe dictates your nervous system's response.

- Shallow breathing keeps you in stress mode.

- Deep, intentional breathing grounds you in presence and clarity.

Everything starts and ends with the breath. Master it, and you master yourself. If it's good enough for Navy Seals, Mystics, and Sages, then it's good enough for you.

Take three deep breaths now...

3. Don't Take Life Too Seriously—Laugh!

Self-esteem flourishes when we stop gripping so tightly to control. Most of the things we stress over are never as serious as we think once we gain a greater perspective.

If you can laugh at yourself and find humor in your struggles, you unlock a deeper resilience.

4. Own Your State—Take Radical Responsibility

Here's a truth that will set you free: The way you feel isn't dictated by circumstances; it's dictated by how you interpret them.

Instead of being pushed around by life, take responsibility for how you process it. If something is making you miserable, ask yourself: "What meaning am I assigning to this?" You always have the power to reframe your experience.

5. Empty the Cup—Let Go of the Noise

Most of what we struggle with is mental clutter such as old stories, outdated beliefs, and inherited fears. Let them go.

When you clear the space, you make room for something greater like true self-esteem, built on love, courage, and wisdom.

Final Thought

By holding back your best self, you rob the world of something extraordinary.

You are exactly where you need to be right now. Step forward. Expand. And enjoy the ride.

"Don't back down just to keep the peace. Standing up for yourself builds self-confidence and self-esteem."

— Unknown

Stronger Than You Think:
Embracing and Building Self-Worth

By Kandi Roemhildt

I stand on the edge of the Gulf of Mexico, the waves tickling my toes as the evening sunset paints the sky with shades of orange, purple, and blue. The rhythmic sounds of the water meeting the shore match my cadence of breathing, in through my nose and out through my mouth. For me, this daily ritual hasn't consisted of just a walk on the beach, viewing yet another sunset; it's been a grounding of sorts, an experience of gratitude, and a testament to me and my journey into self-esteem.

My story began long before this serene evening, in a small town far removed from the tranquility of Orange Beach, Alabama. I was born the oldest child of four into a modest household in Minnesota. My dad was a teacher, and my mom stayed home with us for most of our "growing up" years. While some might think it chaotic to have four siblings, each just two years apart, I remember it as a time of joy and exploration. We lived in the country, where our days were filled with growing food in the garden, doing chores, and experiencing the simple freedom of childhood.

Looking back, I realize how much those early years shaped me. Our home was nestled in the country surrounded by fields, towering pine and oak trees, and dirt roads that seemed to stretch endlessly. Summers were magical. We spent hours playing in the yard, riding our bikes, playing in our tree house, trying to catch fireflies under the starry skies, and splashing around in the nearby creek. Winters brought their own charm, with snowball fights, making snowmen, and sledding down the biggest hills we could find.

But such carefree innocence did not last. When I turned seven, the joy of childhood became overshadowed by darkness, the burden of navigating childhood sexual abuse. The laughter that once filled the air as a young child was replaced by a silence heavy with fear, too vast for a child to understand. The pain and confusion during these formative years left scars, both seen and unseen, etching themselves into the very fabric of my soul. They carved a deep well of self-doubt, unworthiness, and loneliness within me, a void that swallowed my sense of value and safety.

Life became endless mazes of questions with no answers, revealing a world that felt indifferent to my silent cries. Looking back, I can see that the hole in me grew, becoming a cavern of ache and isolation that would take decades to understand and heal. Yet, even amongst these challenges, a tiny seed of resilience was planted in my heart, a fragile hope, buried beneath the weight of it all, waiting to one day grow toward the light.

"You're stronger than you think," a voice would whisper within me. It was faint but persistent. That mantra became a lifeline, a whisper of hope I clung to when life felt unbearable.

My elementary and high school years were challenging, as all preteen and teen years are. Peer pressure, adolescence, and the attempt to maneuver my days around, seeing where I fit in, made every day feel like a tightrope walk. Beneath the surface, I struggled with an unrelenting sense of inadequacy that hugged me like a shadow. The classroom became a stage for endless comparison, where every classmate's success seemed to highlight my failures and reinforce a growing belief that I wasn't enough. Hallways filled with cliques and whispers only deepened my insecurities, each laugh and glance feeling like a blow to my self-worth.

It is amazing how these voices of doubt, of questioning my self-worth and value, seemed to scream through the logical mind. As humans, we latch onto the negative thoughts swirling in our minds before taking a moment to truly see the reality of the situation. It's as if once the negativity starts, it snowballs into an unstoppable avalanche, pulling us further away from truth and clarity.

Even in moments of fleeting joy, an ache persisted—a quiet, constant reminder of my isolation. It was as if I was screaming silently in a room full of people, looking at them desperately, hoping to be seen and understood, yet utterly invisible.

At night, the silence was deafening, a reminder of the void I carried within me. I'd lie awake for hours, replaying every moment of the day, dissecting every word and interaction as if uncovering proof of my unworthiness. Each memory became a magnifying glass for my flaws and failures, amplifying my self-doubt until it was nearly unbearable. Loneliness wrapped around me like a heavy winter coat, suffocating and unrelenting. its weight pressing down on my chest until even breathing felt like a chore. The isolation in my heart grew like a dark, creeping vine, tightening its hold with every passing night. The chatter in my head didn't stop at night. I would find myself listening to meditation music, or running a fan. Anything to avoid the peace and quiet that sleep should give each of us.

The short intentional bursts of self-esteem were induced by self-reflection on books that I was reading. My father was a coach at our high school and an admirer of Zig Ziglar, whose speeches and books emphasized the power of a positive attitude, goal setting, perseverance, and self-esteem. Ziglar believed that building confidence and a strong sense of self-worth was essential to a successful life. I found his work in the early days of the personal development movement, which spurred my interest and established my foundation for seeking positive life choices, personal growth, and dipping my pinky toe in the waters to understand self-esteem.

Even in a room full of friends, laughter echoing around me, I felt like an outsider. I was there, but not really. I was just a shadow of who I was, hollow and hidden. My smiles felt like fragile masks. I could feel that I was playing a game of joy on the outside and pain on the inside. I witnessed friends freely laughing, without a care; meanwhile, the inner voices kept telling me how unworthy I was, how who I was didn't matter. I was ready to crack and crumble at the slightest touch of vulnerability. The ache of invisibility consumed me, whispering cruel lies that my true self was unworthy of love or even to be seen. I longed for someone to notice the storm raging behind my eyes, to reach through the walls I had built around me and tell me I mattered. But the nights stretched on, silent and merciless, leaving me to battle the darkness alone.

Being alone felt safer for me. I used it as a shield against the chaos and uncertainty of my teen years. Avoidance became my survival tactic, and I threw myself into work at age thirteen to escape the pressures and joys of being a "normal" teenager. While others were laughing at parties, going to movies, or having sleepovers, I made work my refuge, my escape from a world I felt I could never truly be part of.

"Oh, sorry, I have to work," slipped effortlessly from my lips, a rehearsed line that kept me at arm's length from others. Great excuse, huh? Each time I said it, I felt a pang of sadness, but it was quickly swallowed by relief. After a while, peers no longer asked me to hang out because they knew my response. It was easier this way, easier to bury myself in tasks, in the mechanical rhythm of labor, than to confront the overwhelming fear and vulnerability of trying to belong. I realized that work wasn't just a job; it was a confidence booster! It gave me a sense of purpose, commitment, and true value. Knowing that I mattered and that the people around me genuinely appreciated my presence really made a difference in how I saw my worth and value.

As the hours dragged on at work, I couldn't ignore the quiet truth gnawing at me. The deep longing to be seen, to be truly known. But the thought of letting anyone in was terrifying. My lack of self-esteem whispered that if people got too close, they'd see the flaws I worked so hard to conceal: the self-doubt, the fear, the quiet belief that I wasn't enough.

Being an empath only made it harder. I craved connection and ached to give, listen, and love without restraint. Yet, I built walls instead of bridges, convincing myself that staying busy was enough. I told myself this was the life I had chosen, but deep down, I knew it was just the life that felt safest. The one where I didn't have to risk being seen and found unworthy.

In my early twenties, I left for college, hoping that a drastic change might mend the brokenness that I was feeling inside me. Moving from a small country town to the "big city" was an opportunity to reinvent myself, to escape the weight of my past, and to be anonymous. But instead of healing the unresolved trauma, I tried to disappear in the collegiate world. During this time, I developed an eating disorder, a desperate attempt to control something, anything, in my chaotic inner world. For fifteen years, I battled bulimia in silence, the relentless cycle eroding my self-worth even further. Day after day I would tell myself, "Okay, today is the last day. Starting tomorrow, I will stop this."

For years, I lived in a vicious loop seeking control in chaos, grasping for validation, and waging an unending war against my reflection. Punishing my body felt logical, and my attempt to control the craziness I was experiencing in my head punished the shell I was living in. The moments of victory were few. I can clearly remember standing in front of the mirror, tears streaming down my face, as I whispered, "Why can't you just be enough?" The scale became my compass, and every number dictated my mood, my value, my place in the world.

And yet, somewhere in the depths of despair, a spark remained. That small voice, the one that said, "You're stronger than you think," persisted. It was faint, but it was there, a reminder that there was more to life than this endless cycle of self-destruction.

Self-esteem is a word we often hear but rarely understand. For me, it is the measure of my value, my sense of worth. On the outside, I appeared confident, composed, even thriving. I was a great actress. But inside—oh, yes—I was my harshest critic, saying things to myself I'd never dream of saying to another human being. This dynamic was relentless, and it took a toll on my spirit and sparkle that I so wanted to have.

One day, a question echoed in my mind: "Who am I to speak to one of God's creations so negatively?" The weight of that realization shook me.

My journey toward self-esteem began with therapy. I would reach out to anyone who I thought might open the doors to my soul and help see what was truly stopping the life that I wanted. In those days, sexual abuse was not spoken of as much as it is today, so paving this path of honesty and vulnerability was arduous to say the least. I sought out a counselor specializing in trauma and spent months unraveling the web of my past. After each session, I would tell myself, "Ok, you got this. You can make it." And then another day would go by without change. Therapy was not a quick fix; it was a slow and long process. Some days, the emotional weight felt unbearable, and I questioned whether I'd ever find peace.

One day, I stood on a bridge, looking down at the cold, lifeless highway below. The voice in my head was relentless, overwhelming: "Jump! No one cares anyway!" But then another voice emerged, quieter yet resolute: "Breathe…just breathe. You're stronger than you think." That moment marked a turning point. I realized that while the negative voice had been loud, it wasn't the only voice inside me. There was still hope.

I discovered yoga and meditation. At first, the idea of sitting still and focusing on my breath felt foreign and uncomfortable. But as I committed to the practice, I connected with my body in a way I never had before. Engaging in activities that uplift me not only brings joy and a sense of accomplishment but also empowers me to see new ways to boost my self-esteem. Yoga became my sanctuary, a sacred space where I could reconnect with myself and rediscover the strength and resilience that had been buried beneath years of self-doubt and pain. Each movement, each pose, became more than just an exercise; it was a celebration of my body and spirit, a testament to everything I had endured and overcome. On the mat, I felt alive, powerful, and grounded, as if the weight of the world melted away with every breath. Yoga wasn't just about flexibility or physical strength; it was a journey inward, a way to honor the parts of me I had once ignored or dismissed.

Meditation became my anchor, teaching me to sit with my thoughts without fear or judgment. I learned to observe the storms in my mind, the swirling chaos of worry, self-criticism, and regret, and let them pass through like clouds in the sky. It was a practice of release, of letting go of the need to control every thought and instead finding peace in simply being. With time, meditation cultivated a profound stillness within me, a sense of calm that I had never known before. The practice showed me that beneath the noise and negativity was a quiet, unshakable core of truth and strength. Together, yoga and meditation became my refuge, my reminder that healing is possible, and that within every struggle lays the potential for profound transformation.

Journaling became another powerful tool for self-discovery. Each night, I would sit alone with my notebook, pouring my heart onto its pages, desperate for some form of release. There was no structure, no plan—just raw, unfiltered emotion spilling out onto the paper in ink-stained confessions. My tears often smudged the words, as if the pages themselves cried alongside me. The notebook became a sanctuary where I could lay down my pain without fear of judgment, a silent witness to the chaos within. Over time, this process helped me build self-awareness, self-compassion, and ultimately, greater self-esteem. By witnessing my own growth on the pages, I began to see my strength, resilience, and worth in a whole new light.

At first, all I could see in my words was the weight of my struggles, memories that burned and fears that suffocated me. But slowly, amidst the darkness, I caught glimpses of something else: a quiet strength, a resilience I hadn't realized was there. The act of writing became a mirror, reflecting not just the scars of my past but also the courage it took to survive. Line by line, I rewrote the narrative of my life, not as a victim shackled by circumstances, but as a warrior, rising from the ashes of my pain. A phoenix of sorts. Journaling wasn't just a tool; it was a transformation, a journey back to myself, proving that even in my most broken moments, there was still hope, still light, still me.

I am realizing in these words that I am the creator of my life. That all of the brokenness, self-doubt, and scars that I had been carrying made me the strong and resilient person that I am; without them, who would I be today? These small insights may seem trivial, but, step by step, they start to build on each other, and confidence starts to attract possibilities. This confidence then directly opens up a shift in self-talk, the inner critic loses power, and I start to hear more self-affirmation instead of self-doubt. This growth in self-esteem attracts a healthier connection with myself because I then start to believe in my worth.

One of the most transformative steps in rebuilding my self-esteem was embracing conscious living. For years, I struggled with self-doubt, questioning my worth and hiding behind the fear of not being enough. I took a leap and enrolled in Redesign Training, a program dedicated to personal growth and self-discovery. Through this journey, I began to unravel the limiting beliefs that kept me small. I learned to silence the inner critic that told me I wasn't worthy, and replaced it with a voice of self-compassion. I started recognizing my value, not for what I could do for others, but simply for who I was. With each lesson, I gained the confidence to step into my power, trust myself, and embrace a life where I no longer needed external validation to feel whole. A life where self-esteem meant recognizing my intrinsic value, feeling deserving of love and respect, and trusting in my own decisions.

On the very first day of the program, the trainer made a statement that stopped me in my tracks: "You are perfect, whole, and complete, just as you are; you are born that way." Those words struck a chord so deep within me that I couldn't hold back the flood of tears. It was as if they had unlocked something buried, something I hadn't dared to touch. The weight of their truth washed over me, overwhelming yet undeniable. I grabbed my journal and, with trembling hands, barely being able to see through the tears in my eyes, began to write the words down, over and over, as though repeating them might etch them into my very soul. Each stroke of the pen felt like a lifeline, a desperate attempt to anchor myself to this newfound realization. I wasn't just writing words; I was reclaiming my worth, breathing life into a truth I desperately needed to believe.

For so long, my self-esteem had been fragile, built on the opinions of others and the fear that I was never enough. But with each word, I was challenging that narrative, breaking free from the self-doubt that had held me captive. I was determined to let this new increased level of self-esteem seep into the cracks of my broken confidence, to heal the wounds of comparison, perfectionism, and unworthiness that had shaped my reflection for too long. Through the tears, I vowed to carry these words with me, not just as fleeting affirmations, but as the foundation of a new self-image. I promised to see myself through a lens of self-respect, to let go of the shame of my past, and to walk into my future with a confidence that no longer depended on anyone else's validation.

I believed I needed to change the very cells of my body to truly embrace who I was. Slowly, I felt the truth of those words on a cellular level. For the first time, I could answer the question of who I was, and I stepped fully into the wonder and grace of self-esteem.

And then, the negative inner voice stopped.

I adopted practices like grounding, breathwork, and mindful eating. These intentional acts reinforced my connection to my body and the world around me. Walking barefoot on the beach, feeling the cool blue water of Florida's springs, kayaking along serene creeks, each moment became a celebration of life and a reminder of my worth.

As I grew stronger, I realized that my journey wasn't just about healing myself; it was about helping others. I felt it to be a responsibility. I began sharing my story, opening my heart in a way I never thought possible, choosing to live boldly from a place of strength and confidence.

I made a decision to launch a business dedicated to guiding others on their journeys of self-discovery and self-esteem. I want to help people see what I had finally come to understand. Every life holds immense value, and every person has the power to create their true potential. This isn't just a business; it is my soul purpose that is born from my heart, a way to turn my pain into purpose. I long to inspire others to step out of the shadows of doubt and fear, to ignite their passion, and to create lives filled with meaning and joy. I see to be a beacon for those searching for their light, empowering them to live boldly, unapologetically, and with the unwavering belief that they are capable of extraordinary things. Shine your light; there will never be another you!

The tools I gained from Redesign Training have become a powerful arsenal in my toolbox that is forever etched in my daily life. They aren't just lessons; they're lifelines, ready to be used whenever I need them. Every morning, I wake up with a sense of purpose and intention, knowing that these tools are more than just strategies; they are keys to unlocking my greatest potential.

Each tool is there for a reason, tailored to help me navigate the challenges of life with courage and grace. For the first time, I truly believe that I have everything it takes to live with self-esteem, to honor my worth, and to embrace my journey fully. These tools have transformed my mindset, empowering me to step into each day with confidence, resilience, and the belief that I am capable of creating the life I've always dreamed of.

Through this work, I've connected with people from all walks of life, each carrying their own burdens, each seeking their path to self-worth and awakening the truth inside of them.

Sharing my story has become a source of inspiration and vulnerability, a way to show others that they, too, can overcome their struggles and create a passionate purpose-filled life.

Looking back, I am struck by how far I've come. My past no longer defines me; it empowers me. The experiences that once felt like heavy burdens now serve as a powerful foundation for empathy and connection with others in this world.

My life isn't perfect, but it's authentic, and that's enough. I know that self-esteem isn't a destination but a journey, one that requires daily effort and intention. I embrace the ups and downs, knowing that each step brings me closer to the person I am meant to be: perfect, whole, and complete.

As the sun sets over the Gulf, painting the sky in the wondrous hues of orange and pink, I begin my walk along the white sandy shore. My footprints mark the sand, each step a reminder of my strength and resilience. Each wave that washes over my toes renews my sense of purpose. I am ready to face whatever life brings, knowing that my journey into self-esteem is not just a destination but a catalyst for a life well-lived. And with every step on this warm white sand, I carry the unwavering belief that I am worthy of deep passionate love, that I can live in joy, and that I will create peace in the world around me.

"Living into self-esteem is not a destination—it's a daily practice of showing up for yourself."

— Unknown

Like The Tree, I Stand

By Magali Dorffner

The late afternoon light filtered through the sliding doors, warm and golden. My laptop sat open on the dining table, a glass of water beside it, drops of condensation trailing towards the wood. The blank page in my notebook waited to carry my deepest thoughts. Simmo's face appeared on the screen, his voice steady and familiar. He had been my coach for a while now, guiding me through the tangled mess of burnout, grief, and self-discovery.

After a short chat, we embarked on a conversation about self-esteem. My body relaxed into the dining chair, my elbow resting on the one beside me. Thoughts swirled in my mind, my words ready to flow like a steady river, until Simmo brought up a quote.

"Like Einstein said, if you can't explain it simply, you don't understand it well enough." A slight smile played on his lips. "So with this in mind, tell me, what is self-esteem to you?"

My chest tightened as I held my breath, thoughts freezing mid-motion, like soldiers halting at the sharp blow of a whistle. The question seemed deceptively simple. After a long exhale, I said, "Okay…" My head tilted back, my gaze lifting towards the ceiling as I searched for the right words. I had spent so much time thinking, reflecting, and living through the highs and lows of self-esteem. Yet now, stripped to its essence, what did it truly mean to me? What clear and simple vision could I now anchor in my heart to always draw upon later in my life?

After a long pause, I finally spoke. "My self-esteem is like a tree."

Simmo leaned in, intrigued. I closed my eyes, gathering the words that had begun to form so clearly in my mind.

"With self-esteem, I am spreading my roots deep into the ground, unshakable and self-sufficient, while reaching my branches high into the sky with confidence and trust. I own my place amongst the trees, feeling worthy and important, contributing to the forest with respect and acceptance, and flourishing in my own light with optimism and strength."

As I spoke, my back straightened, my chest opened, and a quiet certainty settled within me. The words hung in the air, settling in my mind and in my body. Simmo smiled, "That was beautiful."

At that moment, I wasn't just describing a tree. I explained what it meant to be me: proud, grounded, enough. Self-esteem wasn't something you would find, nor was it something external to be earned. It was always inside us, waiting to be recognized, nurtured, and allowed to grow.

* * *

This awareness came much later in life. I never questioned self-esteem or its meaning when I was younger; I was too busy living. Growing up in Vienna, my years as a flight attendant took me beyond Austria and Europe, opening exciting doors to the world. It wasn't long before I fell in love with Australia, quit my job, and set off traveling across the continent for several years with nothing but a backpack, little savings, and a heart full of trust in myself. It felt like a clean slate: new places, new connections, new possibilities. I could be myself without any expectations or pressures.

Two years into my journey, I was still living on the road, now travelling in my rusty 1982 Troop Carrier with my loyal rescued companion, Wolf. I felt free. Free to follow my own rhythm, to wake up each morning knowing the world was mine and nothing would stand in my way. I fully owned my place in this big adventure. I was proud, confident, and happy within myself.

Self-esteem has many faces, and looking back, I now see that period as a time when I felt more myself than ever: closest to the tree of self-esteem, deeply rooted, and moving through life with a deep belief in myself and my choices.

I remember my crossing of the Nullarbor Plain, a vast, unbroken stretch of the Australian outback, with sweat clinging to my back and the sun glaring off the windscreen, baking the endless desert around me. I had no idea what lay beyond the horizon, but that never concerned me. I had no plan, only trust.

That trust extended beyond just the journey. At a remote checkpoint on the Western Australian border, an officer stopped me for inspection. "You can't bring any of this fresh produce across," he said, gesturing to my food stash.

My stomach sank. That was all I had left to eat. With no work in sight for over a thousand kilometers and only enough money for fuel, this food mattered. I pleaded my case, explaining that if he confiscated it, I would be left with half a jar of peanut butter and dog biscuits. But rules were rules.

Without hesitation, I grabbed an orange, peeled it, and took a determined bite. If he wouldn't let me keep it, I would eat it all right there. I worked my way through as much of it as I could—oranges, bread, honey—all while the officer watched, unimpressed. Smirking at myself for my stubbornness, I eventually handed over my supplies. But deep down, I knew I wasn't afraid. I would find a way, just as I always had.

If self-esteem is trusting yourself, embracing uncertainty with optimism, and believing you will be okay no matter what, then I had it in abundance.

But even in those years of absolute freedom, moments of doubt crept in, subtle, fleeting, but real. I had always been confident, yet sometimes I felt insecure. I believed in myself, yet I often sought validation from others. I had no answer to these contradictions and didn't really give it too much thought. Instead, I put it down to my star sign. We Geminis simply have two sides. It made sense, so I left it at that.

I only started diving deeply into the meaning of self-esteem twenty years later when I hit a low point in my life: a point when self-esteem was nowhere to be found.

* * *

One summer day in February, the sun's force, amplified by the absence of the afternoon sea breeze, set the ceiling fan in my living room spinning furiously, stirring up dog hair and dried bamboo leaves that skittered across the floor. Beach sand clung to my damp soles as I sank into my white armchair, its soft cushions patterned with green ginkgo leaves, a symbol of resilience and strength. But I felt neither. Instead, my chair became a place of self-doubt.

Cool streaks traced my sticky cheeks, and a wave of shame washed over me as my eyes traced the surrounding chaos: the clutter in the room, the overgrown backyard, the kitchen bench buried under days of dirty dishes. My beautiful home stood neglected, a reflection of my incapabilities. And I was useless and unworthy of this sanctuary.

Movement in the kitchen caught my eye. A cockroach boldly made its way across a dirty plate and before I knew it, a surge of adrenaline propelled me out of the chair. In absolute disgust, I found myself on a hunt around the grubby dishes. Fueled by the sudden urgency, I emptied and refilled the dishwasher, and my lips curved with a feeling of accomplishment as I wiped down the benches. I stood for a moment, tall and still, a flicker of self-worth washing over me. But as quickly as it came, it faded. The house was tidier, but I wasn't. The mess inside me hadn't changed. Drained, I melted back into my ginkgo chair, my self-worth dissolving into its fabric. I curled up tightly, hugging my knees. Tears welled up again, blurring my vision and my body shaking with sobs that came in waves.

I wished to hear the calming voices of my parents one more time. I was craving the caring embrace of a loving partner who didn't exist, I longed for the cheeky smile of children I never birthed. I yearned for the closeness of my family, far away across the ocean. But more than anything, I longed to feel like I mattered. Never had I felt so alone. So scared. So worthless. So incapable of supporting myself. In that moment, self-esteem felt like a foreign concept, something I no longer recognized within myself.

* * *

How did I end up here after being so independent and successful? My career had flourished, yet I couldn't see how I had spent so many years running on empty, putting work and everyone else before me, neglecting myself for too long. When I lost Dad, then my friend, and almost my dog at once, it was as if the universe had lined up storm after storm, pulling the ground from beneath me. And then, just as I thought I could push through, everything stopped. I had nothing left to give.

I believed burnout had stolen my self-esteem, burying it somewhere unreachable. I told myself I would find it again as I recovered. But to reclaim something, you must first understand what is missing. Self-esteem had always felt like something shifting within me, sometimes strong and sometimes fragile. I now saw it differently: not as one solid thing, but as something made of many pieces, each one shaping the whole like a puzzle. And that made me think back to one in particular.

A memory surfaced—one of my brothers and I at an art exhibition. As we exited the show, he surprised me with a puzzle of a painting by my favorite artist, Gustav Klimt. Over the next few weeks, I spread the pieces across my table, eager to see the image come to life. As I neared the end, the painting came together in all its brilliance, except for one glaring gap. My eyes widened, and my heart sank as I searched everywhere: in and under the couch, inside the vacuum cleaner, even in the bin. But the piece was gone. I stared at the puzzle, beautiful, yet incomplete.

It mirrored my own self-esteem. For years, I had unknowingly searched for the missing piece, outside myself, in others' approval, achievements, and relationships. No matter how stunning the picture seemed, it was never truly whole.

I needed to turn my search inward, to peel back the layers of my thoughts, emotions, and actions. Where were they coming from? What meanings had I attached to them? What boundaries had I built around them? Those questions swirled in my mind, prodding at the foundation of my self-esteem.

The unsettling time of burnout offered answers to my questions. And as painful and challenging as this season of my life was, something inside me whispered, *this is exactly where you need to be.* Forced to stop and put my life on hold, the noise in my mind eventually faded. Thoughts slowed, like leaves floating gently to the ground. What was left was a calm I hadn't known in a very long time.

I was grateful for the stillness. Without it, I wouldn't have reflected as deeply. And without that reflection, the missing piece of my self-esteem would have remained unseen.

* * *

With each passing day, I began to untie my self-worth from everything I had previously attached it to. I would reach for my journal, filling the pages with raw, unfiltered thoughts. Some days, the words spilled onto the paper like a steady stream. On other days, my pen hovered over the page, allowing space for whatever needed to surface. But I always wrote with the same purpose: to listen to myself, understand, and offer compassion where judgment had once lived.

This is how I truly began to live: not doing more, but being more. The stillness that once felt forced became something I cherished. Each morning, I would sit on the wooden deck outside my bedroom, surrounded by plants and the gentle hum of nature. When I closed my eyes, I stepped into a space of serenity, my senses sharpened, and I had clarity in my mind. It felt like gazing into a crystal-clear ocean on a calm day.

Gratitude became part of my morning routine, stretching a smile across my face and filling my heart each time. I first let appreciation rise naturally. Sometimes it was something as simple as the morning sun warming my face or the sound of my dog's breath beside me. These moments surfaced easily. It was the deeper reflection, the gratitude for who I was, for my strengths, and my weaknesses, that made all the difference. It made me acknowledge the beauty not only in the world around me but within myself, in parts long overlooked.

Becoming more than just a practice, it became the lens through which I saw myself differently. For the first time, I felt enough. Not because I had achieved something or met expectations, but simply because I existed. This wasn't a sudden revelation; it seeped in slowly, settling into my bones like warmth from a fire. And with it came a quiet strength; this wasn't just self-love, but self-esteem taking root, anchoring me in my own worth.

One of my brothers once told me the sun rose when I entered a room. I had lost that glow. But as I leaned into being enough, as I lived in that feeling, the glow returned. Even strangers noticed the renewed sparkle in my eyes.

I remember stopping at our beach café on my morning walk with my dog, Bowie. A lady stood behind me in line, and we started chatting. As we parted, each cradling our hot drinks, she stopped me. "Excuse me?" She placed her hand on her heart and said, "I just wanted to tell you what a beautiful person you are. Thanks for that moment we shared."

I didn't need her words to believe it. I already felt it. They were simply a reflection of what I had embodied. I smiled back, not out of a need for validation, but from a place of knowing that I was on the right path, stepping back into my self-esteem.

Being and feeling worthy also led me to confront parts of me I had long judged. My body had changed in the years leading up to and during burnout, and with it, my relationship with myself. I had held myself to high standards, and any deviation felt like a failure, with the weight of self-criticism and shame pushing down on me heavily.

Things changed as I began to embrace my body, not as something to fix or criticize, but as a part of me to honor. Self-love wasn't conditional or tied to a number on the scale; it was about feeling comfortable in my skin at every stage of my journey. Knowing this is one thing; truly living it is another.

I remember a moment when I truly felt this shift. I had been for a swim with Bowie and was walking back to my car, still in my wet bathers, my beach bag slung over my shoulder, my bare feet warm against the pavement.

As I reached the end of the walkway, I stepped into the midst of a wedding celebration with elegant dresses and suits, laughter, and glasses raised in a toast. The old version of me would have shrunk back, self-conscious in my wet bathers, suddenly hyper-aware of how I looked and how out of place I seemed. But instead, I smiled, my body relaxed as I greeted the bridal party, at ease in my skin, unbothered by how I appeared. And with that acceptance came freedom.

Loving and accepting myself didn't mean I surrendered my goals or wasn't working towards something greater. It meant that, for the first time, I wasn't waiting to arrive at some imagined destination before allowing myself to feel worthy. I was worthy now, in this very moment, as I was. And that changed everything.

* * *

Journaling became my space for reflection, the place where I questioned, connected, and pieced together the patterns shaping my life. As I unraveled my experiences, another part of my compromised self-esteem, how much I had attached my worth to others, especially my father, had surfaced again.

Growing up, I never questioned it. Looking back, I now believe that as the youngest in a big family, I had often felt unseen. But as my older siblings moved out and my parents' lives settled, I found myself in Dad's spotlight. I had all his attention and basked in it, treasuring every moment. In my childlike mind, I equated his presence with love, and I feared that if I lost his attention, I would lose his love too. And so, I clung to it. I became his little girl, eager to make him proud, to never disappoint him, to keep my place by his side. Without realizing it, I shaped myself around this belief. I didn't understand how much I had tethered my self-worth to that validation, to the light in his eyes when I made him proud, and how, without it, I felt unmoored.

This pattern didn't stay within our home. Over time, it followed me into friendships, relationships, and my career. I became a pleaser. I agreed just to make others feel good. I swallowed my opinions to keep the peace. I said yes when I wanted to say no. It wasn't a conscious choice; it was the way I had always been. Being easy-going, adaptable, and agreeable made me likable.

But beneath it all, an invisible fear lingered: If I stopped pleasing others, would they still love me? Would I still be visible? Would I still be important?

It wasn't until later, during a hypnotherapy session, that I uncovered just how deeply I had tied my self-worth to others. I had sought out the session because I felt uprooted, lost, and struggling to find myself after moving back in with Dad as an independent woman. I had temporarily left behind my life in Australia, renting out my home and crossing the ocean to be with him before he passed. It was time I had missed out on with Mum. But stepping back into my childhood home after twenty years of independence unearthed old emotions I hadn't expected. The dynamic had shifted, yet I felt myself slipping into old patterns, confronting parts of me I thought I had outgrown.

Under trance, the therapist guided me to recall moments of freedom, when I had felt most like myself. "Collect them like marbles in a basket," he instructed. And so I did. One by one, memories surfaced. Hiking through national parks, swimming with wild dolphins, and driving across vast open roads with nothing but the horizon ahead. I felt free, alive, real.

As I came back to awareness, a smile played on my lips. But then, suddenly, my chest tightened. My brows drew together as I searched for an exception, a single moment that didn't fit the pattern, but there was none. I turned to the therapist, my voice uneasy. "Wait... every moment I collected was when I was alone. What does that mean? That I can only feel like myself when I am completely on my own?" The thought unsettled me.

He smiled gently. "It doesn't mean you can't be yourself around others," he said. As we chatted, I saw it. Maybe, for a long time, I had only felt free from expectations when I was alone. Maybe somewhere along the way, I learned that being with others meant shaping myself to fit them. That discovery sat with me, lingering in the background, subtle yet unshakable. I had never questioned how much I had entangled my sense of self with others, like a spider's web, fine yet solid, holding me in place. But understanding it in theory wasn't the same as living it. I didn't fully confront it until life left me no choice, when my relationship with Dad shifted.

For as long as I could remember, he had been my safe place, steady, loving, and always there. Our bond had always been one of deep love, respect, and admiration. I had placed him on a pedestal, and in many ways, he had placed me on one too. We never argued. We never had to. Until one day, we did.

It was an argument like no other. Not just because it was our first, but because, for the first time, I didn't waver. I didn't smooth things over to make it easier. I stood firm in my own decision, even as it created distance between us. I had spent my life searching his face for reassurance, for the quiet nod that told me everything was okay. At that moment, I didn't get it. The way he looked at me with disapproval, the confusion in his eyes. I felt I wasn't his little girl at that moment; I was someone who had disappointed him and let him down in his final days. And it hurt.

This conversation lingered like an unfinished sentence, the guilt settling in my chest long after he was gone as if waiting for an answer I could never give him. But as I sat in stillness, I could see the argument for what it truly was. It was not a betrayal, but a moment when my self-esteem had risen in a flicker. I had chosen myself, even when it hurt.

My father's love had never been conditional. He had never wanted my approval-seeking ways or my need to please. I had created that story on my own, weaving his opinions into my self-worth like a thread so tightly bound that I had mistaken it for the fabric of who I was. It wasn't just about Dad. It was about me and the invisible patterns I had carried into every part of my life. I had spent so long looking outside myself for proof of my worth, proof that I mattered. But self-esteem wasn't something to be given. It was something to be nourished within.

* * *

That nourishment didn't happen overnight. It required reflection, journaling, and sitting with discomfort to slowly unravel these patterns, one layer at a time. The work was messy. Some days, I felt grounded and strong. Other days, I felt depleted and questioned everything.

In time, I began to understand. Some parts of self-esteem had always flourished within me; the roots I had drawn from throughout my life. Others simply needed strengthening, and my permission to grow. And then there were the parts I hadn't even realized were missing, the ones tangled within a web I had spun around myself. A web that had served me, held me, and felt like home. But it had also quietly suppressed my authenticity, my boundaries, my voice.

Slowly, I stopped shaping myself to fit, and instead expanded into who I already was: unfiltered, unafraid, and enough.

I held my missing piece and gently pushed it into place. I smiled as the puzzle seemed complete, but the smile held something deeper. It wasn't about reaching an endpoint or becoming a finished version of myself, no:

Self-esteem was an ever-evolving foundation for how I lived, treated myself, and moved through the world.

Stepping into it felt like spreading my roots deeper into the ground, unshakable and self-sufficient, while reaching my branches high into the sky with confidence and trust. I owned my place amongst the trees, feeling worthy and important, contributing to the forest with respect and acceptance, and flourishing in my own light with optimism and strength.

And now, as I stand next to my ginkgo chair, the very place where I had once felt so small, invisible, and unworthy, I know I am far from alone and far from incapable. I belong, I matter, and I like who I have become. Like the tree, I stand.

I close my eyes, and he is there. His presence is warm and familiar, just as it always was. "I am proud of you, my little girl." A silent whisper as he holds my hand one last time. He waits for me to loosen my grip and step into self-esteem on my own.

"Merci Papa, je t'aime."

"Self-esteem is not about being better than others. It's about knowing you are worthy, just as you are."

— Unknown

Deserving a Shoulder

———⟨∘◦⟩———

By Kia Stewart

T his chapter almost didn't make it. I committed to contributing to this book during a huge transition in my life. My biggest concern in aligning with the theme was, how could I speak from my experience and deliver the gold that I was still actively seeking? Leaning into self-esteem—what did that mean to me?

The textbook definition of esteem from the American Dictionary is "to set a high value on," or "regard high and prize accordingly" per Merriam Webster. I tried to look back and recall some magical moments when I really valued myself and held myself in high regard, but in all honesty, I've always felt that I've held myself in high regard. I've expected nothing but the best from myself all the time.

No one did shadow work or inner healing better than me. I was such a good coach that I didn't need my own coach; I concluded that since I had already obtained my degree, I could easily be my own therapist and solve all my problems. I know it sounds like I am full of myself, and it's because internally I really am, but leaning into self-esteem isn't just about knowing how much of a "high value" person I am. I have always been one of those people who felt comfortable going to God first. My praise is always "Glory be to God Most High." But when I needed any type of help or support during a challenging time, I consistently struggled with going to God, or anyone, for that matter.

It's difficult to accept that life has both good and bad times, but acknowledging that we deserve help and support can greatly improve our self-esteem. I would like to first start with how I came to accept this uncomfortable truth. There have been many mistakes I have made in my life, but most would never know because I suffered and got through it in silence, hiding my insecurity behind being "private" or holding myself "accountable" for my mistakes. I own every choice I make and will sit with the effects of my actions, but why did I always feel like it was a prison sentence I had to carry out on my own?

I am a single mom to three wonderful children, and many people who see or encounter me on a typical day will say how strong I am. How I am doing an amazing job every day by myself with my children. How I make it look effortless. But the reality is that for a long time, I was barely hanging on by a thread every day. I had isolated myself in a place of solitude until I could find someone perfect to have around my kids. I had already made so many mistakes with men that I made myself a single parent; my "picker" was off, but that was my problem. *I can't complain,* I thought. *Any help that comes along I need to thank the heavens for every day because I shouldn't have to seek support for the children I created.* This was my narrative and I owned it.

Keeping everything under wraps and not asking for help until you reach a point where you have to beg for it, and then overcompensating for any help you receive, is not an example of high self-esteem. This entire thought process had been on repeat for God knows how long, and it was easy to memorize as TV shows, podcast experts, and social media had lots of things to say about single moms. I was told I should simply give up and settle down, become an easy lay because my poor choices had already made me damaged goods, destined for failure because I had already failed to provide my children with a two-parent home.

My intelligence became overshadowed by stupid mistakes that repeatedly caused my downfall. Although I got back up, I dared not ever ask for a hand up or a handout. This narrative deprived me of allowing a community to support me. My day-to-day struggles comprised putting on a brave face, never letting people see me sweat, and acting like a winner even while feeling defeated. As a single parent, it's easy to fall into these traps and not even know that this is how you have been living your life. As my kids 'primary role model, I never really paid attention to the behavior I modeled for them until I was smacked in the face with my own excuses.

One year, I attended another Ultimate Experience Event in Scottsdale, Arizona, and this time, I took my son with me. The room was filled with some amazing people, including ourselves. I was so excited to have my son share that moment with me. He had what I thought was the most amazing time a nine-year-old boy could ever have. He made so many new friends and really embraced the moment fully. As his mother, I was extremely proud because he was always a star to me.

Following that three-day event, I was pumped and I just knew he felt the same, but I couldn't have been more wrong. I received a phone call from his teacher informing me that some kids overheard him sharing with someone that he was going to cut himself because he didn't want to live in this world. As a mother that was the most heartbreaking thing I could ever hear.

My initial thought was, what did I do to make him feel like that, and what could I do to make him want to change? He was my firstborn, who had brought the ending of an old way of life and the beginning of a new way. How did he get to this point in his life, and how did I not already know? After that phone call, I waited for my son to get home and prepared myself to listen with my heart to my little boy.

I repeatedly asked him what was wrong and what was making him feel that way. His response every time was that there was nothing wrong and that he was sorry about what he'd said. Every time he responded this way, I felt like I'd been knifed in the heart. I just wanted to break down crying and beg him not to feel this way, but in that moment, I felt the need to be strong and put together a plan on my own. I started going through notebooks he had and found some excerpts from what I thought were times he had been enjoying himself, moments when he received awards and told me about them but was truly sad, caught in a cycle of low self-esteem.

One of the things I gathered from my son was how he idolized me and how sad he felt. I reached out to his doctor and a therapist, and a family caseworker got involved. It frustrated me at times how good my son was at downplaying his feelings. I had to say something. I had to call it out for what it was, and his response hurt me to my core: "I don't feel like anyone would understand me, and I should be able to figure this out on my own. I'm sorry that I made a mistake, and I will do better."

My baby had learned that entire response from me. I had taught him how to put on a brave face and taught him that since folks just wouldn't understand, it was up to me or him to handle it. This realization is one of the hardest I have ever had to come to because serious consequences would result if I didn't stop what I was doing. I had no clue how to get past this with him or for him, but I knew one thing for certain: he was always watching.

It was time to lean on a village, but I had no idea how to do that. I came from a family of strong women, many whom had raised their children on their own or were the heads of their household. Our family motto was often, "What goes on in our house stays in our house," and that was the same message I sent to my son, not through words but through my actions.

We had experienced some really low moments as a family, but I would bite my tongue, grit my teeth, and drag myself through the mud to get through it. I would decline help along the way because I wasn't sure how I could repay it, or I was too embarrassed to even receive it. I had to reprogram my mind, but these lessons would be difficult; I was used to sharing my accomplishments and gifts but dreaded sharing what I considered my burdens.

I first tried small subtle ways, like asking for prayers via posting on social media but not delving much into what was going on. I had people reach out to me with genuine concern. My initial reaction was to downplay it as not a big deal because I was disgusted with how I had created this reality for my child. But, immediately after that thought, I heard my son's voice again: "I don't feel like anyone would understand me." I realized it would help if I raised my self-esteem to be someone who rises above the feelings of shame and releases them. I needed to accept that I was worthy of support and deserved the very best life offers. Our current circumstances are a direct reflection of how we feel about ourselves.

I couldn't solve my child's need for healing because we were both limited by our identities. So, I shared a bit more with an old high school friend who had reached out. She shared with me that she had gone through a similar situation with her child, and instantly my walls crumbled a bit more. I didn't feel so alone. I didn't feel so burdened. *Here is this woman I look up to who understands me and doesn't wish to judge me but simply holds space in love for me and my child.* She became a confidant and a source of inspiration, reminding me that this too would pass and that I didn't have to figure it out on my own.

I have always considered myself a naturally loving person, but I really felt like the Grinch whose heart grew three sizes that day, not from the expression of my love but from receiving it from people who cared. Opening up has been the best thing I could ever do for my self-esteem, and it has created a space where my child is opening up. He has spoken about his struggles and has opened up doors for support to creep in. As a parent, support is something I couldn't ever imagine him not being able to have. I will go to the ends of the earth and back for my son to know that he is deserving of all my love—the love we expect from our parents, who love us both when we're good and when we're bad. I am that unconditional warmth for my son.

I saw a glimpse of my low self-worth on my nine-year-old son's face. I had always been my child's biggest cheerleader but never recognized how much he didn't really share with me. Life isn't all about the high moments, and sharing our wins isn't the only way to share in love. Anger, sadness, grief, and confusion are all natural emotions that not only deserve to be shared but also deserve to be explored. I deserve this, not just for me but for my son and for anyone else who may hear me, see me, or never encounter me at all. What I have to say matters What I feel is valid. I don't have to go at it alone.

I could have fed into the belief that I had to figure it all out on my own and refrain from seeking any prayers, support, or help with my son. But that could have cost his life, and that is a harsh reality I would face to get me on track to being the best, most authentic version of me. I can be vulnerable and know that it is okay. I never have to feel embarrassed because I am loved. I may not know everything, but I've learned to accept and embrace what I need. As a parent, I am important to my child but also to myself. If I hold myself in high regard by asking for help, he'll do the same. My son has been my biggest teacher on raising my self-esteem. It truly takes a village, but as my grandmother used to tell me, "A closed mouth doesn't get fed."

Even in completing this, I can't tell you how many times I have cried in sharing this part of my life, as it is still fresh for me at this moment. I am so glad because being loved and holding space for others to love my child and to love me has been the most eye-opening experience of my entire life. I deserve to feel seen, heard, and loved. This truth that is mine is his as well. We all deserve it. People naturally love and need to be loved regardless of life's circumstances. Love is essential to healthy self-esteem.

We must live our given lives fully and share them with others, good or bad. This entire ordeal gave me just a small glimpse of what God must feel like. God's pursuit of us, going to great lengths to show His love and that we are always worthy, isn't about stepping outside a comfort zone. I believe God created me, loved me enough to give me life, and sent Jesus Christ to die for me, a sinner. Whether you are religious or not, the story of Jesus is the ultimate testament of love and speaks to the ordeal I went through with my son.

This experience gave me a small glimpse of how God could do such a thing. I would do anything for my child to see and know just how much I love him, not for any special reason but simply because he was born.

I did not have to experience a physical death as Jesus had to, but I would go through this ego death every time. Death to the idea that no one will understand, that I messed up and need to simply just be better, or that I am carrying my cross or my burden alone. I can understand that love only because I opened the door to allow it. And the door didn't open just for me; it opened for my entire family.

My son has become more open to sharing with me and has even connected with a coach he met at the Ultimate Experience who shared a similar experience with him. Seeing the light return to my son and life to his eyes has been the greatest reward. I share his sentiment; it can be lonely in our shadows so much that it's easy to get lost. But in the same way, we can be a light to others.

In concluding this passage, I want to share my truths: I am a Human Being, I am a single mother, never married, and am over the age of thirty with three kids. Life gets tough for me some mornings. I get so tired I don't even want to get up. I've struggled with bipolar disorder since being diagnosed in 2010. Sometimes I feel like life would be easier if I were normal. I lost someone extremely close to me, have experienced a lot of heartbreaks, and have sometimes just wanted to break down in tears and ask for a hug. The version of who I was would have only acknowledged all of those statements, followed by a "but" and whatever strength I wanted to highlight, despite things. I have learned that all those attributes and experiences can exist as areas of my life for which to seek support; that doesn't take away my strength but strengthens me. Acknowledgment was the first step in raising self-esteem for me and for my child, who has learned through my actions to lean on me and others as well.

Leaning into self-esteem isn't only about shining in the world but also about how we can still deserve to be shined upon. It's okay to ask for help or encouragement or even just a hug. Letting our hearts speak through tears, joy, or laughter is the greatest gift we can give to ourselves and to the world. We are all deserving, and when we acknowledge this, then we open doors for love to come into our lives.

"Self-esteem grows when you choose yourself over and over again."

— Unknown

A Garden in Bloom: Nurturing Our Self-Esteem Growth

By Manuela Lipp

"We are not the drop in the ocean, we are
the entire ocean in a drop."
— Rumi

I am a soul consciously creating and experiencing life. I am Oneness and Unity. I am nothingness and creation at the same time. I am Yin and Yang. I am here to tell the story of life.

Therefore

I Am love
I Am joy
I Am interconnectedness
I Am growth
I Am power
I Am a creator

My gifts serve you to see who you truly are. I see you and I love you. I am you, and you are me. We Are. Together, we let miracles happen. Let's dance to the music of life. It is not about me; it is not about you; it is about Us. If you grow, I grow, we grow.

We live—we are Life.

We love—we are Love.
We create—we are Creators.
We dance to the music of life.

My wonderful parents named me Manuela. I am here to serve
humanity and raise the level of consciousness.

Therefore, I am a powerful leader and the most transformative
executive and leadership coach in the world. Three years ago,
thinking and even sharing the above statement would have been
impossible. Those words are not born from arrogance or external
validation but from my being. They come from an inner place of
wisdom, of trust in life and love for myself.

For me, living into self-esteem is a journey of rediscovering our true
being and realizing that this alone is enough. It always has been, and
it always will be. It is about recognizing that we are not the drop in
the ocean, but the entire ocean in a drop, as Rumi so beautifully
said. As little kids, we don't doubt who we are or what we are
capable of. But there is one challenge: we get "socialized." We learn
how things work and how they must work on the outside. We
develop strategies to make life easier for us. But as we expand on
the outside, we often forget to stay connected with our inner world.
I believe connection to the inner self is essential for our self-esteem.

School Time

Attending school as a child was quite easy for me, even though
sitting around all day didn't always feel right. During elementary
school, I decided I needed to go to secondary school and then
university. I don't know where that idea came from, but it became

clear that this would be my path. It would be a way for me to prove to everyone that I was a worthy member of society.

Well, I struggled to get into secondary school, having to take the entrance exam three times before passing. But there was just no other option. I had to go to secondary school and prepare for university. Looking back, I now see this period as a defining moment. Even though the "failures" shook my confidence, they also taught me perseverance.

At fifteen, just before entering secondary school, I decided I would do an exchange year at some point. I remember feeling strongly about it: "This has to happen. It is important for me." I can't tell you what inspired me. It was probably something I read that made me dream about how fantastic it must be to travel abroad for one year. Trust me, it wasn't easy to get my parents to agree to this proposed adventure, but they finally did because they knew I would grow immensely after the experience. I am still very thankful that they made this possible for me! At seventeen, I travelled to Australia and stayed with a wonderful family for a year. Leaving the country where I had grown up was a wonderful adventure and it gave me a deep understanding that wherever I go, there can be a fulfilled life. But only if I am open to it.

Why do I write this? I struggled a lot during my first months in Darwin, Australia, and showed real arrogance towards some people, especially one of my host sisters, whom I love dearly today. You're probably wondering what that arrogance looked like. I thought I knew everything better and believed I deserved more than being in Darwin. This attitude made me closed off and unable to listen properly to the people around me. I didn't see them.

During that year, I kept a diary. Rereading it later, I realized that what I thought was arrogance was just deep insecurity about who I was and how I should interact with people. That fear made me shut down. And this wasn't the only time in my life that fear had influenced me. Looking back, I realize how often that fear shaped my actions. Fear led me to a lot of "what ifs," overthinking, and loneliness throughout my life.

Looking back, my biggest takeaway from that time was that I could achieve things when I put my mind to it and take action in the direction desired. Doing so might not always seem easy at first, but taking action against all odds or feelings of fear is an important step for me to live into self-esteem.

What experiences shaped you when you were growing up? How do those experiences, no matter if they were good or bad, shape your life today in a positive way? What are you deeply thankful for? When was the first time you had an awareness about self-esteem?

Taking Control of My Career

When I returned from Australia to Switzerland at age eighteen, I finished secondary school and decided, at the last minute, to study law. Yes, last minute! I had no plan for my life and figured I should choose something that would give me a safe job, a good income, and recognition. Plus, I was fascinated (in a scary way) by the idea of studying law, reading all those books on what people called a very dry subject.

At the beginning, I struggled a lot and barely passed my first exam. But I grew into the routine step by step, and amazingly, I even enjoyed combining all the knowledge I had studied. My final exam in law school went well, or at least much better than my first one had. I followed the classical path: training at a small law firm and then applying for the bar exam. At first, taking the bar exam wasn't on my radar. To be honest, I was scared—terrified. In my mind, failing would have meant losing recognition. But then I thought: "Wait, I made it through university, and I improved over time. I even learned to study efficiently. My brain seems to function well. Shouldn't I be able to pass the exam?" I risked it, but not without a solid plan.

My plan was simple: study hard (but not too hard, overdoing things never helps), work on my attitude, and stay convinced I would pass. I told myself repeatedly that 50 percent of success was about how well I prepared; 30 percent was about how I felt on the exam day and how I approached those long hours solving cases; and 20 percent was pure luck regarding the topics that came up. With this logical plan, failure seemed impossible.

It worked. I had a great written exam and passed everything on the first try. What did I learn? When we combine action with the right attitude, we can expand our limits and succeed. And by expanding our limits, we grow into self-esteem. Passing the bar exam was a turning point for my self-esteem. It taught me I could overcome my fears by taking consistent action.

One specific thing that helped me most was focusing on the result I wanted to create and the action I could take to achieve it. I figured out that the work had to be done on two levels: studying and mindset. Fear and doubt came up. Of course they did. But I did not let them take control. My mindset was programmed to win this game!

Can you recall an adventure that scared you at first, but you decided nevertheless to take the risk? No matter if you succeeded or failed, what did you experience and learn thanks to this adventure? How did it shape your personality in a positive way? Where did it make you strong? How did it grow your self-belief and help you develop your self-esteem?

The Turning Point

After years of working as a lawyer in various roles such as consultant, in-house counsel, and head of legal and risk, I had achieved everything I thought I wanted. I was recognized as a lawyer and earning good money. I was a well-functioning part of society. But… Do you know the feeling of having everything you've ever "dreamed" of and still sensing that something is missing? You don't dare say it out loud. After all, you are fortunate to have great opportunities in life. Yet, over and over again in my thirties, I felt that something essential was missing. This realization hit me deeply at forty-one as I lay in bed one evening. I realized that neither my career as a successful lawyer nor my harmonious marriage was truly fulfilling. It was time to move on, but to what?

This realization was one of the hardest truths I've ever faced. On the surface, I had everything: a stable career, a loving marriage, and recognition from others. But deep down, I felt disconnected from myself. My self-esteem, I realized, had been built on external achievements and approval. Without those external reference points, I didn't know who I was or what I truly wanted. This realization was both terrifying and liberating. It was the moment I understood that self-esteem must come from within, not from the roles we play or the validation we receive from others.

My Journey into Self-Esteem

My journey began long before I made the big decision to change my life. I had followed a "safe" path, but deep down, I knew something wasn't right. My work was interesting and time-filling, but it wasn't satisfying. I had already started searching in other areas.

When I was thirty-one, I tried to meditate by myself. But I felt far too impatient to sit still on my own. Instead, I took one course, then another, until a few years later, I completed training as a meditation teacher. Did I do something with it? No, not even meditating for myself. But I learned there was another journey waiting: the journey into the inner world, into a world—a state of being—that can't be explained by our five senses of seeing, hearing, smelling, tasting, and touching.

By the spring of 2017, however, I had almost forgotten about my meditation experience. I occasionally practiced yoga and tried to make it a daily routine, but not to deepen my inner journey. The practice was more of a way to function better externally. Yet I kept asking myself questions:

- Why can't I be happy with the life I'm living? Why is there this emptiness within me?

- Is this all there is? Is that how it is meant to be?

- What is wrong with me that I just can't be happy and enjoy life?

Our self-esteem may not be at a very high level if we face these deep-down questions, doubting everything done so far because the feeling beneath is not right.

Finally, I attended a coaching retreat. It was three days in nature filled with deep conversations and insights. Everything clicked. I realized I wasn't living from my heart. Rather, my life was being led by my brain and what I thought others expected of me. I knew it was time to go in a new direction. But how?

My first step was terrifying: I left my marriage to another beautiful human being. I didn't leave because of him, but because of me. Shortly after, I quit my job as a lawyer, despite the safety it provided. Looking back, I know I could have been gentler with myself, but the urgency for change felt overwhelming. And to be honest, I felt quite lost, not knowing where this path would lead me. Somehow, I knew from past experiences that everything would turn out right. But how could it when I didn't really have a plan, and especially when I felt messed up? How would I know which direction to take? What if, in the end, I was just crazy and not worthy?

To "free" or "calm" my mind, I had the most intense love affair of my life. I traveled to India for a yoga teacher training, and then spent time in Sri Lanka, South Africa, Australia, and Indonesia. Somewhere along the way, fear crept in again, and I accepted a new legal job in Switzerland. It seemed like a step back into safety… but I had an idea! While working again as a lawyer, I began my first coaching training. The focus on solution-oriented systemic therapy opened my eyes to the possibilities of change. I understood that transformation starts with awareness and the courage to take just one step. Looking back, these were the most important steps in living into my self-esteem. I learned to recognize that no matter what is happening on the outside, "I can always be the master of my inside."

Here are the key insights from my journey:

- **We are shaped by patterns, but we are not defined by them:** I discovered how much of my life had been guided by unconscious patterns. Often, these strategies had developed during the first seven years of my life. What helped me the most was realizing that other people were struggling in ways similar to mine.

  That realization encouraged me to look closer at my life and see that it was okay not to feel okay. It was okay to struggle. Slowly, things shifted (really slowly; it seems that I like to take my time). Step by step, I came to understand that it was normal for us to be influenced by patterns and that some, while once helpful, no longer serve us. Those patterns didn't define me; they were just stories I had been telling myself.

  Discarding those patterns wasn't easy for me. I remember being the client during a coaching training and discussing a challenge in my life. My inner dialogue went something like this: "I have everything under control. I don't have challenges. Everything is fine. I am fine. I stand above it. I'll just pick something small." But here's the truth: the small things can reveal the most, and in the moment it happens, we might not feel very happy about it.

Acknowledging this felt a bit like being caught, which did not have the best effect on my self-esteem, realizing how little I knew about myself and how my world actually worked.

I discovered how much I thought I was in control when, in reality, I was floating unconsciously, kind of blind, clinging to the illusion of control. But what can we do about that? In my experience, the first steps are being aware of what exists, understanding how we are shaped, and accepting this without self-judgment. Strong self-esteem doesn't come from pretending to have everything figured out. It comes from being honest with ourselves and accepting what exists without judgment.

What really helped me to stop judging myself was the realization that I was experiencing something completely normal for a human being.

When you notice a pattern, a certain mindset, or a reaction to something, these two questions might be very helpful to you:

o   *"Where did I learn this from?"*

o   *"Does it elevate my self-esteem?"*

- **True leadership starts with yourself:** I faced real challenges when I started my new job in 2019. Leading people wasn't easy for me, and my insecurity caught up with me.

Here's a secret: You can't lead others if you're not first the leader of your own life. True leadership begins within. For me, it was about recognizing my worth and taking responsibility for my growth and decisions. For years, I was constantly seeking to belong, to be enough. That need was so deeply rooted, I didn't even know it, until I did.

One day, I discovered that deep down, I didn't feel worthy. By realizing this, things shifted. I embraced it. I stopped depending on others to validate my worth. Instead, I started focusing on who I am. The way I wrote that makes it sound easy, but getting there was difficult and it took me a long time.

A lot of things in my life, especially in my profession as a lawyer, were created based on a need to belong. I searched for belonging and confirmation on the outside. They were the motor and fuel for my career as a lawyer, which, don't get me wrong, I am very grateful for. I wouldn't be who I am today without traveling that career path. But, looking back, I realized why it took me so long to gain insight about this mindset/pattern ruling my world. I needed this mindset/pattern to be my motor, and the wonderful thing is that I took a lot of precious and useful skills with me from that time.

Are you aware of a mindset/pattern that drives you most in your life? Is there a mindset/pattern you learned as a child that you've carried with you? Is that pattern still helpful or does it hold you back? Ask yourself how this mindset/pattern was and might still be helpful to you. Do you believe you are worthy?

- **Self-esteem and growth are intertwined:** Self-esteem isn't something we achieve once and for all; it evolves with us. I experience growing into self-esteem as waking up to my true self.

  Growth happens when we expand our understanding and embrace the adventures and experiences life offers or has already offered us. For me, this has meant understanding that something was missing and then seeking my truth, challenging myself to see the world and myself differently.

  Each experience in my way added resilience, understanding, and confidence. Growth isn't about leaving a "comfort zone"; it's about realizing that the boundaries we experience are self-made.

  What boundaries do you experience in your life? Ask yourself if they are rooted in truth—must they still be present or would a shift in your thoughts and understanding open up different possibilities? Who would you need to be and what would you express in this world, having no limits or harmful learned beliefs?

- **Everything begins within—the importance of growing into self-esteem:** True self-esteem isn't found in achievements or external validation. It's found in simply being and in shifting our perspective on life as a human being. I had a big insight on this theme during a transformative "Be With" session with life coach Steve Hardison. I realized that everything I was searching for was already within me. Steve made me write the sentence that came to me: "Being in one's own being is such a safe and simple place."

From this place of wholeness and oneness, everything feels possible. An insight like that may fade away a bit, but something shifts permanently, opening the door to new possibilities, understanding, and growth. I'm not anywhere near the end of my growing, but I know deep down that I've started waking up, and this process can't be stopped anymore. I have this deep inner knowing that life presents me one possibility after another to expand and grow.

With that, my life has adopted a richness which I have never thought possible. I see my outside world as a mirror of my inside. If I see something go "wrong" on the outside, I go in search of my wisdom within and ask myself what lesson is to be learned for my further growth. Or, in the more positive way around: when I'm drawn to something or someone, I follow the call in curiosity of what this encounter has installed for me.

Trust me. There is no more room for fear, only for adventure and exploration of the world. Although, I have to be honest. I sometimes have thoughts of fear, but I just don't follow them or let them have control over me anymore. I now honor and believe in my worth as a human being.

Is your world or life created by external circumstances that you hardly react to, or are you consciously creating your life? Where do you stand on your wonderful journey as a human being? Are you living in your own being or are you chasing a role or idea of someone else? Do you believe in your value?

Growing into self-esteem brought me face-to-face with many insights about myself and about life. It wasn't always easy, but each step provided new insights and deeper clarity. The lessons I learned were not just about breaking old patterns or finding my worth. They were about learning that everything I needed was already within me and there was no reason to be afraid of anything. That wonderful saying by Rumi finally made sense.

Tools for Growing into Self-Esteem

Maybe growing into self-esteem doesn't happen overnight; maybe it feels like a journey of deliberate steps. But sometimes it might even be just a thought away. Over time, I've discovered tools and practices that have helped me reconnect with my true being, break free from limiting patterns, grow into self-esteem, and start waking up to who I truly am.

You don't need any special training to use the tools below, just curiosity, a willingness to explore, and the courage to take action. The most important thing is this: be gentle and loving to yourself. Forgive yourself for everything that happens. You've always done the best you could with the thoughts and mindset you've had. Love yourself unconditionally. You are a soul creating and experiencing life!

- **Become aware of your thoughts:** Our thoughts play a crucial role in shaping our reality. Noticing your internal dialogue is one of the simplest yet most profound ways to transform your life and grow into self-esteem. I discovered how often my thoughts were self-critical or fear-driven. By observing these thoughts, I could question them and choose new thoughts that reflected my true worth.

  I invite you to pay attention to your inner dialog. Are you gentle and loving to yourself, as you would be to a dear friend? Start observing your thoughts this week. Notice when they uplift you and when they limit you. What is one thought you could replace with a more empowering thought?

- **Discover your values—your inner compass:** Values can help create the foundation of a fulfilling life. They have the power to guide your decisions, align you with your true self, and bring clarity to what matters to you.

  When I finally connected with my values, I realized how often I had ignored them in favor of what others expected. Recognizing my values became a turning point in my journey. They are now the center of my self-portrait, which you read at the beginning of this chapter. I have created a guideline for discovering one's values.

- **Practice gratitude:** Have you ever heard the saying that gratitude is the fertilizer for making our dreams come true? Gratitude may very well be the first step toward growth into self-esteem. By embracing and being grateful for what is, we strengthen our vibration for beauty and for ourselves.

Studies have found that whether you are grateful for something simple or something big, your level of happiness is the same; the brain doesn't really know the difference. It is all about the feeling you want to capture. And a good feeling within you leads to a different view of the world. It raises your sense of belonging and self-belief. Possibilities open up where you might have been stuck before. To practice gratitude, you can integrate the following simple but effective practice into your daily routine: take some time every evening to reflect on the things you are grateful for.

Write down three things from your personal life that you are grateful for. Next, write down three things from your professional life, and then three things about yourself. It doesn't matter if they are small, big, or happened during the day or over the past few weeks, months, or years.

Conclusion of My Journey

Growing into self-esteem is not a destination; it is a journey. It unfolds moment by moment as we reconnect with who we truly are. Along the way, we have the chance to let go of the misunderstandings that have kept us small and step into the truth of our being.

When we live into self-esteem, we might start noticing how our relationships improve and how we see possibilities that were hidden from us before. But we don't just transform ourselves. Along the way, we might even inspire others. Our growth creates ripples, showing what is possible and uplifting those around us. Self-esteem is not only a gift to us but a contribution to unity, joy, and shared growth.

The moment we take one small step toward self-esteem, we nurture the garden of our true being, realizing it has always been within us, patiently waiting for our care and attention to bloom.

"To be yourself in a world that is constantly trying to make you something else is the greatest accomplishment."

— Ralph Waldo Emerson

Building Self-Esteem:
A Pathway to Healthy
Relationships and a Fulfilling Life

⊸∘⌒⌒⌒∘⊸

By Phil Barlow

I opened my heart to a woman in a way that revealed a sensitivity within me that I didn't even know I had. I gave all of myself, including my love, time, energy, structure, kindness, and care. In this openness, she said, "I hate you, and you're making me hate your music." I never expected such a harsh response, but it would become a turning point in my understanding of self-esteem, inner balance, and the power of healthy boundaries.

Music and family are the two most important things in my life, and she knew how important they were to me. She later apologized and explained that what she was really trying to say was that things were going too fast, and she needed space to integrate and grow.

I did my best to release those words, but the truth is they rolled around in my mind for days. That single sentence cut deep, forcing me to question the relationship, how and why it got to this, and my responsibility in this situation.

I thought I knew what self-esteem was until I had the wind knocked out of me.

Perhaps you will relate to the struggle as I share some of my stories or at least get a glimpse into the depths from which I have learned to build strong and resilient self-esteem. So, to those with wavering self-worth (or difficulty reaching goals), I wish to pass on how I navigate this in the hope it will help you avoid the pains I have experienced and live a fulfilling life.

After years of trial and error, I discovered that building strong self-esteem hinges on three core practices. Each step builds on the last, guiding you to honor your values and protect your emotional well-being. They are:

1. Get clear on your values and what your best life looks like (vision).

2. Establish healthy boundaries (with safe communication and appropriate consequences).

3. Move forward with confidence and trust.

Let's begin...

I ran into love with the belief that if someone truly cares about me, I can open my heart completely, and they will care for it, receiving my loving gestures as I do my best to take care of theirs.

I ran into love, compelled to open the heart of a woman, to feel that surrender from her, but I had no idea what it takes to actually hold a woman in that vulnerability.

Both led to an incredible amount of heartache, dysfunctional relationships, abusive behavior and self-esteem that swung from overconfidence to a lack of confidence and withdrawal.

I have been married and divorced. She was a wonderful woman, and we had all the things of an Australian dream, but we became deeply unhappy and I walked away from it. It left me lost and confused for many years, trying to understand what happened. Fourteen years later, I am finally getting it. I am learning about unhealthy attachment and the ways I was overly dependent on her to feel loved, to feel happy. I was also giving from a place of self-sacrifice.

I now understand it is my responsibility to know who I am and what I value and make sure I honor that in my life decisions. If I am unhappy, it is my responsibility to learn from my mistakes, to reconnect within, and make better choices.

It all seems so simple to write it, but the truth is I have been in a world of emotional hurt for so many years, looking outward for a cure to an unquenched heart.

I had other significant loves, which started with rich romance and passion until they became deeply intimate. Then they would become emotionally unstable, marked by constant pushing and pulling of love and support, and I never truly felt settled.

* * *

I've lived through some pretty traumatic experiences in terms of relationships and abusive behavior, which I'm not proud to say.

I ask myself: Why did I tolerate this? And also, why did I behave that way?

I suppose I didn't really understand the subtlety and depth of what was happening unconsciously, nor how it was affecting my self-worth. I also didn't know how to get out of the toxic cycles that were occurring and what was causing them.

How did I change this? I took responsibility for my situation, for my choices, and for my role in it.

I discovered that living with self-esteem is about creating a way of life in which my thoughts, words, choices, and actions are aligned with, support, and protect what I truly value.

Releasing Victim Mentality

Victim mentality is the sense that everything is happening to us rather than the belief that we can influence our life circumstances. When we see ourselves only as victims, it's difficult to create lasting change.

How does it feel to be a victim?

It's horrible. It feels demoralizing and helpless. It's the "why me?" reality. From this perspective, it's hard to enact change. It's okay to feel that way; it's actually healthy to feel the hurt and anger and then transform it into action that creates safety for yourself (with care for how it affects others). You can then move forward in the direction that honors your self-worth, self-respect, and integrity.

Taking Responsibility

What was my role in it? And why did I keep choosing to re-enter an unhealthy relationship?

What I opened this chapter with is my side of the story. The other side is the way I was behaving, unconsciously, in relation to the other person. I was moving fast with tight timeframes and high expectations. I got frustrated when I was being misunderstood. I got angry and raised my voice. I withdrew from the relationship abruptly when I got triggered, sometimes staying disconnected for days.

We had full-on fights until we were exhausted from emotional ups and downs. She told me she didn't feel safe expressing herself and that she was walking on eggshells. They were just words to me at the time; it didn't really make sense. I showed up to every conversation with good intentions.

Did I feel good about the times I was triggered and how I reacted? No. It was not aligned with my heart or with how I want to treat people. The way I behaved lowered my self-esteem because it wasn't aligned with my values.

After years of struggle and emotional instability in my relationship, I had those closest to me asking, why are you tolerating this behavior, and why do you keep going back?

I didn't have the answer, and I had to take time and space from the relationship to let that unfold. My simple answer was that we had a deep love, but the reality was that it was not a safe and healthy relationship. How did it get to this? Why Did I stay in that situation? Was I contributing to it?

I had an unhealthy attachment style. We both did.

I wasn't grounded in my own values, and while I was living a pretty good life, there was a deeper layer of my core values for peace and music that wasn't being reflected in my decisions. The result was that it affected my self-trust, and I would then look outward for answers, outward for love, and outward for emotional stability.

So when my relationship would go up and down, my whole inner world would become destabilized. I was seeking something from the relationship that can only truly be found by being deeply rooted in my own being, trusting my intuition, knowing what is important to me, trusting my judgment, and trusting life. In other words, feeling secure in myself first, and then enjoying the connection and passion of intimacy.

Secondly, I was rushing through life.

I was so focused on achieving goals and ignoring my inner state of stress and anxiety. Upon reflection, I see how the way in which I was achieving goals was affecting my well-being, my relationships and my overall enjoyment of life. I needed to slow down, to trust in the flow of life, and the richness that comes with simplicity and connection.

It's so easy to blame another, or adopt a victim mentality, but the truth is the real growth occurs when we take responsibility for our choices, ensuring that our own behavior and that which we tolerate, aligns with what we truly value.

Once we are living in alignment with our values, it then unlocks the depths of self-acceptance, self-love, and the ability to experience peace and joy.

Values, Vision, Boundaries, and Trust

When it comes to building self-esteem, we begin by identifying what truly matters to us, our values, and imagining how we want those values expressed in our daily lives. This is our vision. Through my experiences, I have learned that people are inherently different in what they value, in what it looks like to have those values fulfilled, and in how they behave to get their needs met.

Each person must be clear on what is important to them, communicate it *in a safe way*, and maintain *healthy* boundaries that protect those values.

When boundaries are knowingly crossed, there need to be *appropriate* consequences that are followed through. Children need this, and adults do as well. It enables close relationships in which both people can live with self-esteem.

In this way, you can feel good about yourself, relationships gain the resilience and structure to build trust and flourish, and you can move forward with confidence.

Values – What Is Most Important to You?

Sometimes, we need to be crystal clear about what is most important to us so we can make tough choices as we move forward. Values help us discern the moments that call for flexibility versus those that call for strength.

Your values are your personal guidance system. They give you a reference point to align your thoughts, words, and actions in creating your best life.

Everyone is different. Even people who share the same values may have different perspectives on what it means to embody those values in daily life. Therefore, clear communication of your values is equally important.

If I am living in alignment with my core values, then (and only then) can I truly feel good about myself (self-esteem) and trust myself. As I trust myself on a deeper level, I can trust and surrender to the flow of life, to its constant change and abundance, allowing myself to experience peace and joy.

What are your values?

If you had to narrow it down to the five most important values in your life, what would they be?

Mine are... *Peace, Creative Expression, Family, Respect and Honesty.*

(There are many tools available online to help you get clear on your values, and I encourage you to set aside time to do this.)

Then, within those values, get clear on exactly what it looks like for you when that value is being reflected in your relationships and lifestyle.

Example: Respect

1. Listen to the experience and wisdom of elders and trusted peers.

2. Value other people's time and effort.

3. For myself, honor/value my time, energy, experience, and wisdom.

4. Care for the hearts of others; don't tolerate disrespectful behavior.

This process is helpful because what I perceive as "respectful" and what another person perceives as "respectful" can be completely different. With a higher level of awareness about what you value, it becomes easier to communicate with others and to set healthy boundaries.

Self-esteem has its roots in how we feel about ourselves and our lives. By connecting regularly with what is most important to you and learning how to communicate and protect what you care about, you strengthen your self-worth and feel empowered to move forward.

Vision – Creating Your Best Life

Where are you heading? What does it look and feel like to live your best life?

What are your relationships like?

A vision is creating a clear picture of what you want. A great vision aligns with your values and inspires you to take action. It is the bigger picture that drives you through challenges. It is also a way to realize once you have attained it to enjoy it!!

As I sit here in this moment, I acknowledge the many facets of my life that are really fulfilling to me. I have a wonderful lifestyle; I am healthy, I have great relationships with my parents and sisters, good friends and a supportive community, and lots of great music around me, coming through me and on the horizon. I have much to be thankful for, and I have worked intentionally to create this life.

There are also parts of my life that are not yet as I envision them. My previous relationship caused me a lot of heartache. Did I have a vision for it? Yes, I did. We tried for many years to materialize a shared vision, but the emotional stability was not there, and the peace was not there. Through the experience, I was forced to get real clear on what was important, and in this case, to make the tough choice of letting go when things went beyond challenging to an unhealthy and unsafe situation.

The vision I have for my close partnership is one of harmony. A calm, loving relationship where each person feels at home, can express and receive what is important to them, and enjoy the experiences of life together. Right now, I am working on the relationship I have within me, with a vision to experience peace and joy first, and then open to sharing it with another in an intimate partnership.

Action Steps: Once you have arrived at your core values, create a vision for what your life circumstances and experiences look and feel like when these values are expressed in your outer world.

There are many ways to do this, such as a vision board, a mind map, or a written statement. Whatever works for you. It's the big picture that inspires you, and in simple terms, it becomes your "why" that keeps you focused through life's ups and downs and to learn when to say no thank you.

If my self-esteem is low, I check in with my vision to reconnect with my "why" and realign with what is important to me. I connect deeply with my vision and direction at the change of each season, and I embrace New Year's Eve as a ritual to refine my vision for the year ahead.

Once you have done this, you now have a structure that builds resilience into your self-esteem. But how do we safeguard what we value in everyday interactions?

Healthy Boundaries, Safe Communication, and Appropriate Consequences

It was only recently that I found myself in a situation where it seemed everyone around me was behaving in ways I was not okay with. I didn't like how I was being treated, and the way I responded seemed to make things worse. The person I deeply loved was behaving in emotionally abusive ways and repeatedly crossing boundaries. A festival organizer was overtly disrespectful to me in front of my partner. My stepchild was glued to a computer screen at a time we had set aside to connect as a family. The point is that there was clearly something I needed to learn in order to feel good about myself and about the types of interactions and people I had in my life.

I needed to learn how to set healthy boundaries, how to communicate them safely, and how to assert consequences when boundaries were crossed.

I learned about boundaries the hard way: both by not having strong enough boundaries (and tolerating abusive behaviors that were not okay) and by having unhealthy boundaries that were too rigid, communicated reactively, or accompanied by consequences that were too harsh for the behavior.

A boundary is essentially the threshold that defines what is okay and what is not okay with you.

What makes a boundary healthy is how it is communicated and the presence of an appropriate consequence.

My self-esteem and how I feel about myself are related to what I tolerate and to how I treat others in relation to my deepest values.

Asserting Boundaries

Through my choices, I assert my boundaries; through my words, I assert my boundaries; through my actions, I assert my boundaries.

Physical boundaries can be easier to understand, like a fence between two neighbors. It clarifies where the boundary lies. Some physical boundaries are more nuanced, such as when, where, or if it is okay for someone to touch you. Perhaps you're okay hugging your parents but not okay with a hug from someone you just met.

Psychological or emotional boundaries can be more challenging. In my experience, I have learned where my boundaries or thresholds lie by noticing how I feel in certain situations. It's also possible to create boundaries consciously and adapt as you live with them. This is what I am currently learning to do.

Either way, the point of communicating a boundary is to let people know what is and isn't acceptable to you. As relationships become more intimate, getting to know and respect each other's boundaries is crucial for each person to live in alignment with their values and enjoy positive self-esteem.

When it comes to enforcing consequences if your boundaries are crossed, it's important to make sure the consequence is appropriate (not too extreme or too insignificant) and that you follow through.

Ideally, it will be the minimum consequence needed to shift the behavior and protect what you value. This creates a safe pathway for relationships to grow closer as each person gradually learns how to respect and care for the other's values.

If your boundaries still aren't being respected and consequences aren't effective, it may be time to take more significant action, such as removing yourself from the situation and creating a life that aligns better with your values.

I encourage you to dig deeper into healthy boundaries and safe communication. This is my current area of growth, and I'm excited about the closeness I am experiencing in my family relationships and the positive effect it's having on my self-esteem.

Moving Forward with Confidence and Trust

When I create space to get clear on my next move, and it aligns with my deepest wishes, I honor myself. It is a process that embodies self-respect for my time, energy, money, and purpose in this world.

As I emerge from those inward phases, I move forward with clarity, vision, goals, and inspiration. I also strengthen my self-esteem and inner drive. I have stepped into my personal power to activate my best life and higher purpose.

Now, as I face challenges, I trust that these are the right challenges for me. They connect with my values and my heart, and they are worthy of all my intelligence, passion, and power.

I am all in, fully immersed in life and this precious, dynamic, abundant, fragile, and beautiful human experience. Of course, being committed brings its share of trials, leading us to explore further.

Fulfillment and Challenges

The difference between fulfilling and unfulfilling achievement is how aligned it is to what you truly care about. Can you see the connection? Alignment leads to fulfillment, which leads to high self-esteem (feeling good about yourself and your life).

This doesn't mean there is no challenge. It means the challenges are worth it, and the energy to face them is available to you, one way or another.

There are subtle energies at play that go beyond willpower and a strong mindset. When we truly trust ourselves and know we are living authentically, we can open ourselves to all the support and grace that is available.

Choice – Asserting Self-Worth and Reinforcing Self-Esteem

If we have no choice in a matter, it can feel restrictive or suppressive. This feeling has fueled me many times to work hard to position myself so that I have choices.

It started by taking full responsibility for where I was, getting clear on where I wanted to be, and having the courage and discipline to work at creating that reality.

On the other hand, having too many options or potential life pathways can create confusion, overwhelm, and procrastination.

Then there are the "fork in the road" moments, when we know that the choice we make will significantly affect the direction of our lives.

In such moments, I am learning to be cautious not to let my mind slip into a victim mentality, looking outward for a person or situation to blame for why I can't make the choice I want or need to make. The mind does this to avoid pain (i.e., if I make the wrong choice, it could be painful).

This can lead to giving away our power of choice to the influence or opinions of others. Then, if it doesn't work out, there is someone else to blame. In the end, you are the only one who knows the right choice for you.

Do I approve of my choice?

I believe this is the single most important question for making a commitment that is true to you.

So, what if I took full responsibility for my life, for my choices, for my directions, and for my unfolding reality?

I must choose wisely, and once I commit, I must follow through and back myself completely. Ironically, if I make a choice and then move forward with hesitation, it only undermines my self-confidence in decision-making and lowers my self-esteem.

Know yourself, and take ownership of your life's direction by committing to the choices that are right for you.

The Art of Saying No

Life is full of opportunities, needs, and wants.

If you lack discernment, you may find yourself constantly responding to the needs and wants of others, often to your own detriment. To maintain strong self-esteem, you must have clarity about what is worthy of your time and energy. This allows you to say "no thank you" when you do not feel valued in an exchange or when you have other priorities that are more aligned.

When I make such choices, I feel centered and empowered. My choices determine the life I create for myself, and if I say "yes" to things I don't believe in or that don't honor my sense of respect, it weakens my self-esteem. It happens subtly, bit by bit, a lack of discernment can creep in until the life we live no longer reflects the life we truly want.

So, why is it difficult to say "no thank you?"

Guilt

We are wired for social connection and belonging. It is a primal instinct that serves as a survival mechanism, enabling us to co-regulate each other emotionally in times of stress and protect each other in danger. For this reason, fears arise whenever a situation could threaten our connection or sense of belonging with friends, family, or community. Unfortunately, some people exploit this instinct to get what they want.

The important thing to remember is that we can choose who we spend time with, which relationships we invest in, and what life we want to build. Sometimes, it means pushing past feelings of guilt to say "no" and remaining firmly connected to your values. Trust yourself as you embrace change and build a better life.

Sometimes, the people and situations around you respond to your discernment with mutual respect. Current relationships deepen, and life circumstances develop in ways that align with who you are.

- *Low self-esteem comes from making choices that undermine what is truly important to you.*

- *High self-esteem comes from making choices that align with what is truly important to you.*

Cause and Consequence

In the physical world, a basic law of cause and effect is always at play.

If you drop a stone into a still pond and then decide you'd like to enjoy the still water, you must wait until the ripples have dissipated.

It is the same with life choices and actions: The stronger the action (cause), the stronger the result (consequence).

If you have spent years living out of alignment with what is important to you, it's wise to cultivate patience and remain open to deep transformation and healing.

By being fully present in your current situation and realigning your choices to your values, your physical reality will eventually reflect what you truly hold dear. It's inevitable. If it doesn't happen instantly, recognize that the "karma" from past actions is still dissipating.

Be proud of where you are heading and the work you are doing to build your self-esteem while extending compassion toward your former self. It is only by becoming conscious of our thoughts, words, and actions that we gain the power to change.

Conclusion

Living with self-esteem is an ongoing practice. Life weaves in mysterious ways, and now more than ever, our modern world is fast and complex.

Still, we have the power to create inner stability in our lives. It starts by taking full responsibility for the reality we are experiencing. Once we do that, we embark on a journey of self-discovery that leads to building a genuinely fulfilling life.

By getting clear on what is most important to you, it becomes easier to prioritize and make decisions. Having a clear vision of what your best life looks like establishes your "why," giving you strength, drive, and direction.

As you move forward, the healthy boundaries you create and your conscious efforts to communicate them safely will nurture your relationships, making life more supportive. If boundaries are crossed, you assert appropriate consequences to protect what you value.

In this way, you can live a life of peace and fulfillment. Take one concrete step today, such as clarifying your most important value and visualizing what it looks/feels like in daily life, and watch how it begins to uplift your self-esteem.

May your deepest dreams come alive.

"You must find the place inside yourself where nothing is impossible."

— Deepak Chopra

Learning to Value Myself

By Leigh Huxley

"**S**trong self-esteem helps us navigate the worst storms and teaches us to appreciate the light at the end of the tunnel even more."

* * *

Emily loved spending half term at her grandmother's house out in the countryside. She lived in the city with her parents and would visit during school holidays. Her favorite afternoon activity was reading a chapter from Winnie-the-Pooh and reciting a quote at the end.

"Granny, what does Pooh mean when he says 'the things that make me different are the things that make me, me'?"

Watching the rain trickle gently down the windowpanes, the grandmother answered, "We all go through experiences in life that shape us and make us the unique individuals we are. We all have strengths and good qualities, and we all have limits, that will test our self-esteem. How we think and feel about ourselves is not set in stone and can be changed. We can't change events, but we can change how we see them. To be ourselves in a world constantly trying to make us someone else is a great accomplishment. Come, I want to show you something."

She took Emily lovingly by the hand and led her into the lounge where a glass display cabinet stood proudly. Reaching up to the top shelf, she carefully removed a beautiful old vase that had been repaired several times. She allowed Emily to run her delicate fingers over it.

"Why have you kept this, Granny?"

"Because it reminds me of my journey of self-esteem and how it shaped me. Would you like to hear more?"

"Yes, please. Can we make some hot chocolate and sit by the fire while you tell me?"

"That sounds like a wonderful idea!"

They made their favorite hot chocolate and got cozy in front of the roaring fire as nightfall settled in. The grandmother quietly reflected on her life as she watched the flames dance in the fire-grate.

"I grew up like an only child in a very adult world. I was serious and reserved, the youngest of four, and a surprise to my mommy and daddy. My sisters and brother were much older and had already left home when I arrived. My granny and grandpa lived with us, and my grandpa was my main playmate. There were no children my age where we lived. I watched the adults go about their daily lives and took on the belief that life was a serious affair, fraught with responsibility and problems I had to solve by myself.

"Although I felt alone in the adult world, I wasn't lonely. I learned to be happy and content with my company, which ultimately stood me in good stead for later in life. I got sent to play school when I was four 'to teach me how to get dirty' and to learn to interact with children my age.

"The ballet teacher introduced me to ballet shortly after I started handing out pamphlets. Unable to read, I excitedly handed my mommy the pamphlet when she fetched me, asking what it said. It was a full-bodied *yes!* from my four-year-old self when she told me. Ballet became my passion, teaching me the joy of movement, confidence, self-expression, self-discipline, and poise. It made me feel free, alive, and unstoppable. Then, one day, five happy, carefree years suddenly ended when I was told I had to give up ballet. We were moving and my daddy was going to become a minister. I remember feeling deeply disappointed, but I accepted the situation because it was out of my control."

"What happened to your granny and grandpa if you had to move?"

"My grandpa had died the year before when I was eight and my granny not long after that. I was heartbroken when my grandpa died. It felt like a piece of my heart was lost."

There was a long pause as they both stared silently into the flames of the fire.

"What was it like to be a minister's daughter?" Emily asked, breaking the silence.

"Very different. I had to start a new school and learn to make new friends. My mommy and daddy had to be careful with money, so I quickly learned not to ask for things I wanted, like I used to. I didn't want to put pressure on them. I felt like a goldfish in a bowl with nowhere to hide.

"There was a lot of pressure on me to be on my best behavior and be perfect all the time, both at church and school, especially after being chosen as head girl of my primary school. The only time I felt I could let my hair down and be myself was when I was with my best friend and her family from church. I spent a lot of time with them as my mommy and daddy were always out helping and supporting people at church with their problems. I didn't mind being part of a larger family, but it made me feel unimportant.

"I took on the incorrect belief that other people's needs were more important than mine and that I only deserved my mommy and daddy's time and attention when I had a problem that needed to be solved. I learned to be small, not to take up space, and to avoid asking for support for fear of taking attention away from others more worthy of it.

"This pattern of feeling insignificant and not speaking up about my needs would thread its way throughout my life until I came to realize that I mattered, my needs mattered, and I deserved to feel good about myself."

"Granny, did you go to the same school as your friend?"

"Not at first, but I could choose whether I wanted to attend the same high school as her after leaving primary school. A few months into our second year of high school, my daddy got transferred to a different church, so I had to say goodbye to her. It was hard, but I think it was harder for her. My daddy used to say that the only thing in life we can be sure of is change, and he was right.

"We can't control everything in our lives, but we can control our choices and how we show up for ourselves. We never know what's around the corner, so that's why it's important to cherish every moment."

"How did you show up for yourself when you went through all the changes, Granny?"

"With kindness and patience. I learned to think kind thoughts and to speak kindly to myself. Having a good relationship with ourselves is very important. How we treat ourselves sets the foundation for treating others and interacting with the world around us. I learned to be adaptable, focusing on the things I could change and seeing the glass as half-full instead of half-empty. I also learned to embrace, not be afraid of uncertainty, and to go with the flow.

"Life's not so scary when we learn to trust and believe in ourselves and the bigger picture. Everything always works out for the best. We're always taken care of and we are never alone.

"Doing hard things helps us to believe we can cope with the changes and challenges of life. It strengthens us. We're never given more than we can handle, always remember that," said the grandmother, hugging Emily.

Emily started to yawn and rub her eyes.

"It's way past your bedtime. Let's get you up to bed."

The grandmother tucked Emily into bed, tenderly kissing her on the forehead.

"Night night," she whispered. "Sleep tight. Love you."

"Love you too, Granny," said Emily, snuggling under the covers.

The next morning, Emily bounced out of bed and ran downstairs to find her grandmother in the kitchen.

"Granny!" she exclaimed excitedly.

"Well hello, sunshine. Would you like some pancakes for breakfast? I've just made them so they're nice and warm."

"Oh, yes, please. Granny, can you carry on telling me your story when I'm finished?"

"I can," the grandmother smiled. "How about we bundle up nice and warm and go for a walk in the woods when you're done? I will tell you more of the story."

Emily eagerly finished her pancakes, found her coat and shoes, and declared that she was ready.

"Well, let's go, then."

"Which way should we go today, Granny?"

"Mmm," hummed the grandmother, wondering how to enhance Emily's belief and trust in herself. "Let's play a little game. Stop for a moment and close your eyes. Take three deep breaths and put your hand on your heart. Keep breathing in and out from your heart and just listen."

"What am I listening for?"

"A small, still voice, almost like a whisper in the wind. You must be silent to hear it, though, and when you do, you must trust it. It's called your inner voice. You can do this any time you don't know what to do. Hear anything?"

"I think so. It said to go this way." Emily skipped merrily down the path that forked to the right, leading them to a beautiful woodland area filled with early spring birdsong. "What happened after you had to move away from your friend, Granny?"

"Oh, it was much harder than the first time. I was a teenager. My body was changing and I didn't like the way I looked. My skin had broken out badly and I felt ugly, self-conscious, and very insecure about how I looked.

"The school year had already started when I joined my new high school, and everybody had their friendship groups. The teacher made me stand in front of the class and introduced me as the new minister's daughter. I felt embarrassed, awkward, out of my comfort zone, and I just wanted to disappear. I wished I had a Harry Potter invisibility cloak! But I put on a brave face and tried not to show how I felt.

"I soon realized that others felt awkward around me, too. They didn't tell jokes or use bad language in my company and would often whisper and giggle behind my back. I felt unwelcome and excluded, but did my best to be friendly and polite and not take their behavior personally. I gradually made a few friends, but I only had one good friend. We had fun together and I would often go with her to her family's holiday home on the weekend. They were wealthy, but I don't know how happy they were.

"Things sadly took a turn for the worse for my friend when her father suddenly died. We remained friends, but not best friends, as I met my first boyfriend shortly after. I was fifteen. He was the youth leader at our church and five years older than me and I found my sense of self-worth and self-esteem skyrocketing to think that someone so much older than me found me interesting, intelligent, and valued my company."

"Did you marry him?"

"I did, but I will tell you about that later."

"Were you clever at school?"

"I was a good student. I worked hard, got good marks, and didn't fail anything, but I had a near miss in my mock exams in my final year. I had studied hard for all my subjects but had left my maths revision too late and couldn't fit it all in. I had a meltdown the night before the exam and spent all night sobbing in my mommy and daddy's bed, hoping they would feel sorry for me. I wanted them to say I didn't need to go and take the exam the next day but, to my dismay, they insisted I did. I was petrified of failing!

"Something surreal happened when I got to the exam hall. It was like a blanket of peace descended on me and I became incredibly calm. I realized I had already done the hard part of showing up and that it didn't matter what marks I got. I failed the higher grade but passed on the standard grade. But, more importantly, I had faced my fear of failure and realized I was more competent and knew more than I thought. It was a hard lesson, but certainly a character-building one that taught me to believe and trust in my abilities."

"What happened after you finished high school, Granny?"

"I chose not to go to university because there wasn't anything I wanted to study, other than marine biology. I didn't want to be a teacher or a nurse like my sisters. I decided that although marine biology would be interesting, it wouldn't be practical as a career.

Then one day, I saw an advert for health and skin care therapy and my heart lit up. It had all the subjects I loved and I knew it was just right for me. It was a misunderstood career choice in those days. I still remember one of the girls in my class asking if I didn't think it was a waste of my brains. Her response surprised me but I didn't let it sway my decision to follow my heart.

"I worked hard and was awarded top Theoretical Student, but it was a challenging, character-building year on many fronts. I remember feeling like I had aged a hundred years by the time I had finished. I was exhausted and my skin was horrendous from all the stress. My self-esteem was in shreds and I loathed the way I looked. Plus, I was about to get married a few months later at the tender age of nineteen."

"Was it Grandpa you got married to?"

"It was. We moved shortly after that to a different part of the country for his first job."

"Did you find a job, too, Granny?"

"I worked for a few small salons before owning my own business when I was twenty-one. I hit a big identity crisis before that, though. I doubted whether I had chosen the right career. I was the youngest of all our new friends and the only one without a university degree. I didn't feel good or clever enough in their company and decided I needed to go to university. I would have studied to become a doctor but that wasn't available, so I chose optometry, which involves the eyes.

"I still remember the day I got the letter to say I had been accepted and, instead of feeling elated, I found myself questioning my motives. I realized I was allowing my insecurities of not feeling good enough to drive me so I immediately phoned the university to say I wouldn't be attending. I decided to embrace my career choice. If people looked down on me because they didn't understand what I did, that was okay. I knew how hard I had worked."

"I'm so proud of you for doing that, Granny."

"Me, too," the grandmother smiled. "We are all as unique as our fingerprints and should never compare ourselves or seek approval, recognition, or praise from others to feel valued or worthy."

"Did you know how to be a business owner?"

"No, but I knew how to be a good health and skin care therapist. I had done hard things before. I had learned to believe in myself and my abilities, and to not be afraid of trying something new. I knew I would be guided to what I needed to know when I needed it. I threw my heart and soul into working in and running the business, expanding it, and moving premises several times.

"I enjoyed the relationships I developed with clients but didn't enjoy dealing with staff issues. I was very hard on myself and expected myself to work the same hours as my staff and run the business. My perfectionism pushed me to nearly burn out by the age of twenty-nine. I hadn't realized how much I had been over-extending myself, putting everybody else's needs above my own and giving from an empty cup just like I had seen my mommy do.

"My life had become completely out of balance and I realized that if I didn't make drastic changes, I would be in big trouble. I started carving time out for myself. I joined a gym, gave myself and my staff an afternoon off each week, took adult ballet classes and even learnt to go onto my toes! I learned to have fun, laugh at myself, and not take life so seriously. The stranglehold of perfectionism gradually loosened as I learned to value myself for who I was and not for what I had accomplished."

There was a long silence before Emily asked, "So where does my daddy come into the picture?"

"Well, I didn't think I could become a mommy. My body wasn't working very well because of all the stress so Grandpa and I decided to see a specialist doctor. I had what they call fertility treatment to help me fall pregnant. It was very hard on my body, cost a lot of money, and didn't work. To make things worse, all my friends were falling pregnant and having babies and that old familiar feeling of feeling excluded, unworthy, and not good enough returned. I was heartbroken."

"So, if that didn't work, how did Daddy come along?"

The grandmother thought long and hard, wondering how she could explain the complexities of infidelity and betrayal in relationships. "The story gets a little complicated. I got caught up in what they call a love triangle whilst I was still married to Grandpa. We had a dear friend who was single and part of our friendship group at church. He was Grandpa's best friend and came to stay with us whilst Grandpa was away for work. He was a bit of a loner and I was drawn to his sensitivity. We would have wonderful conversations and our friendship deepened over time. We fell in love.

"Our relationship went on for a few years but only became physical towards the end. And then, surprise shock, I fell pregnant with your daddy. I was very scared, but told Grandpa about our secret relationship and that I was pregnant. It hurt him deeply. I felt a lot of guilt and shame for betraying him, but I had also betrayed myself. We decided to stay together and raise your daddy as our own. I had to say goodbye to my beloved, which was by far the hardest thing I had ever done. My heart was broken and my self-esteem was shattered. I hated myself. I was deeply sorry for all the hurt I had caused but also incredibly grateful for the gift of motherhood.

"I was petrified of losing your daddy as a punishment for what I had done. Only a few people knew the full story, and I kept the secret for a long time. Your daddy was five or six years old before I told my best friend.

"When your daddy was a year old, an opportunity came up with Grandpa's work to move countries. I had already sold my business, so there was nothing to hold us back. It was a chance for a fresh start, away from all the secrets and lies. But, as I discovered, we take ourselves with us wherever we go and the secret came with me. I found myself still hiding behind the mask of guilt and shame, even though no one knew me.

"Then when your daddy was eighteen months old, we got moved again. We settled quickly and made a lot of new friends from different countries. It was an exciting time and we had a lot of fun. But, as the years went by, our friends moved back to their countries, and I found myself alone again. I felt stuck in the day-to-day of life.

"Grandpa was traveling a lot and your daddy had become unwell with Lyme's disease. It was a difficult and uncertain time carrying everything on my shoulders. I felt stressed, empty, and emotionally unsupported. I was juggling a lot of balls looking after your daddy, running the PTA at your daddy's school, and doing a diploma course. I felt like I was dying inside despite all the busyness.

"One day, I started talking with someone in one of the gym classes I attended. We had both been members for many years but had never crossed paths. We became friends and our friendship grew over the months, turning into a relationship. We both felt unseen in our marriages and found comfort, companionship, and love in each other's company. I knew it was wrong but didn't want it to end. All the inner conflict, guilt, and shame of betrayal came flooding back and my skin erupted like a volcano. What was wrong with me that I found myself in yet another love triangle? I hated myself for the pain and hurt I was causing and was deeply afraid of what people would think and say about me. My inner critic had a field day!"

"Was that Grandad, Granny?"

"It was," said the grandmother, smiling warmly. "Grandad got divorced, and I made the difficult choice of leaving Grandpa. It was a very raw, difficult, and messy time for us all, especially for Grandpa and your daddy. We moved in with Grandad, including Buster the dog, leaving everything behind except for our personal belongings and my car.

"Grandpa and I divorced a year later, and Grandad and I got married when your daddy was thirteen. I was the only one in my family to get divorced, the black sheep as they say, and was very afraid of what people would say about me. My fragile self-esteem had shattered yet again. I found navigating blended families challenging and I found myself in a different type of triangle called a drama triangle. There were three of them and I was the piggy-in-the-middle, trying to play peacemaker in them all. I was afraid of and disliked conflict so I avoided it at all costs.

"I hadn't developed the skill of standing up for myself so I found myself absorbing the conflict instead of confronting it. It devoured me from the inside out and I developed a self-soothing coping mechanism called dermatillomania, a big word for skin picking. I would spend hours at night when Grandad was working extracting impurities from my face. It felt satisfying at the time but I would be wracked with disgust and shame the next morning when I saw the devastation I had caused. I would then spend ages trying to cover it up with makeup to hide it from Grandad and others.

"I realize now how much I hated myself and that I was punishing myself for all the hurt I had caused. There is always deep pain and self-loathing beneath addiction. It went on for a long time and affected how I showed up in the world.

"Then, when your daddy was fifteen, he went overseas to live with Grandpa and his new family and to finish his education. It was a bit of a shock because it all happened so quickly. He had only been gone for two weeks when he had what they call a psychotic break. I didn't even know what that was and I felt like I had been thrust into a different planetary system. Grandpa managed to get him back home to me but it was a long and scary journey to get him back on his feet. I handled the crisis but hit the wall once his medication kicked in and he shut down. I decided I needed professional help and found a psychologist. I told her about your daddy and eventually plucked up the courage to tell her about my skin picking. She did her best to help me but later decided it would be better for me to see someone else, warning me that there was a waiting list of up to a year.

"I decided I couldn't carry on like I was and had to do something about it. Enough was enough. It was time I stopped abandoning myself and giving my power away. I took responsibility for my choices and actions, stopped playing the victim and addressed my negative beliefs and self-talk. It took a lot of perseverance, resilience, and a new puppy, but I managed to turn things around and rebuild my self-esteem one step at a time. I reconnected with my spiritual self through regular meditation, self-reflection, and inner work. I slowly gathered the broken pieces of my shattered self-worth and self-esteem with gentleness and kindness. I forgave myself for all the times I had given my power away by putting other people's needs and opinions before mine, for disappointing people, for being afraid of conflict, for feeling like I didn't have a choice, for doubting, hating, and punishing myself, for the guilt and shame I had allowed to consume me and for wanting someone else to tell me I was okay just as I was when I was the one who had to accept myself."

The grandmother stopped dead in her tracks and exclaimed, "I've just suddenly realized that there's one thing missing that would put the finishing touches on the story of my journey of living into self-esteem and the vase. Would you like to help me with it when we get back home?"

"Ooh, yes please, Granny. Let's hurry home as quickly as we can!" said Emily excitedly.

Once back home, they went to the attic where all the arts and crafts supplies were kept and found some gold paint and the finest paintbrush they could find.

"What are we going to do with all this, Granny?"

"You'll see," said the grandmother as she went to fetch the vase she had shown Emily the day before.

She invited Emily to sit on her lap at the kitchen table. Holding Emily delicately by the hand, she dipped the tip of the paintbrush into the paint and carefully etched the repair lines of the once-shattered vase with gold.

"Look how beautiful that looks. Now, let's promise ourselves that whenever we look at the vase, we will remember the importance of valuing, accepting, and appreciating ourselves," said the grandmother, hugging Emily whilst admiring their handiwork. "We must embrace our past because it brought us to where we are and who we are today."

In Japan, they call it the art of Kintsukuroi, which means "to repair with gold." The broken pottery is repaired with gold lacquer and it's understood that the piece is more beautiful for having been broken.

Self-esteem can't be bought, but it can be built from within.

Only when we have enough self-esteem can we truly develop self-confidence in the world.

"Progress, not perfection, is the path to self-esteem."

— Unknown

Self-Esteem Our Birthright

———— ∽o⟡o∾ ————

By Piera Maria Fromm

How did I get here, and how can I get out?

D ark thoughts crossed my mind: "I wish I would break a leg, or something would knock me out. I need a rest from all this."

I was already diagnosed with chronic fatigue syndrome, and hives were breaking out all over my body regularly. I was no longer comfortable in my skin. I had lost all sense of connection to my body. My mind was filled with negativity towards myself and others. I was suppressing my emotions. It was almost like I forgot what it meant to feel.

At the same time, I had so much anger inside of me.

Anger towards myself for letting it get this far—how could I?

Anger towards my ex for co-creating this situation—how dare he?

Anger towards life—this is not what I envisioned.

To sleep, I relied on smoking a fair amount of marijuana. Still, I was putting on a lovely dress and my makeup every day, masking what was really going on inside me. Putting on a happy-go-lucky facade to the outside world. I was good at it; I pulled it off. So caught up in my misery, I could not see a way out.

It was at that very moment, during one of my lowest points in life, that I decided I was worth so much more.

"I am worthy of living a fulfilling, joyful life. Desiring to get to know myself again, find my authenticity and purpose, and, more than anything, allow myself just to be so I can regain my self-worth."

Promising to myself: "I will make a change right now."

I found the first glimpse of my self-esteem and realized nothing was more important than my own self-worth. No one else will make the change for me. No one else can. What an aha moment that was for me. It finally clicked. Repeating to myself, "No one else can. I am in charge of my happiness. I am the creator of my reality and have much more power than I think." So, my journey of reclaiming and remembering my worth began.

Let's take a step back. How did I get here, and what does self-worth even mean to me?

At this point in my life, I genuinely believe we are all born whole and complete. Every one of us is meant to be here, otherwise, we wouldn't be. We are a vessel of love, with love flowing through every cell of our being. Self-esteem, self-love, and self-worth are our natural states of being. Deep inside, we know how to be loving, kind, soft, tender, and full of power simultaneously. With ourselves, and from this place, we will also treat our surroundings in this manner. Whole and complete, simply for who we are, not for what we do or achieve in this life, but just for our natural state of being.

What goes wrong?

Why do so many of us find it challenging to love ourselves?

Why does our sense of self-worth often seem to be missing?

We treat ourselves with hardness and become very destructive.

We feed our bodies with food that doesn't nurture it.

We don't dare to feel our emotions, so we suppress them.
Eventually, they manifest in our bodies as pain and disease.

We have forgotten how to still our minds and are constantly on
overdrive, repeating the same thoughts over and over, and most of
these thoughts are negative and judgmental towards ourselves.

We don't even hear the voice of our intuition.

Most of us seem to lose the ability to listen to our internal guidance
system and inner compass, which can lead to the loss of our spark
for life. Our spirit dims and our life force seems to evaporate. We
get stuck in a rat race, suffering from loneliness and a lack of
connection to others, and, many times, covering it all up with some
kind of addiction.

As a society, we're often pitted against each other, and it's rare to see
genuine celebration of someone's success; instead, we're filled with
envy and jealousy. From a very young age, we're told that we need
to work hard in this life and strive for success.

But the car we drive, our house, and our financial security measure
this success. The more we accumulate the better. Our actual
happiness or holistic well-being are hardly ever mentioned. From a
young age, the benchmark is being faster, smarter, and well-
behaved. Authenticity and individuality do not seem to be

encouraged. It's quite the opposite. We are expected to fall in line, not stand out, and behave. We are indoctrinated with fear and scarcity; as a result, the world feels unsafe.

And don't get me wrong, I do not see the world as an evil place; quite the contrary, my reality is filled with beauty and magic, and I could not be happier to be alive. I am a true believer that, by changing ourselves, we can make a huge shift in this world. While I have experienced this in my environment for a long time, I have now been able to create quite the opposite.

I was not immune to my surroundings or society's expectations, and for a long time, they robbed me of my self-esteem. Let me share more about my personal journey. I hope it inspires you on your own path to reclaiming self-worth.

I consider myself one of the lucky ones. I am fortunate to have been born into a loving family and raised between two small towns on the opposite ends of the world, Switzerland and New Zealand. My two brothers and I spent most of our childhood in nature, playing with our friends and coming home to freshly cooked meals, always greeted with love.

My memory of my parents while I was growing up is that they were both very hardworking. My father's father died of cancer when my father was only thirteen years old. My grandmother, an exceptional, amazing woman, somehow held on to the business and raised her five children as a single mother. It didn't come without a fight, as during these times, they wanted to place a guardianship over her, calling her unfit as a widowed woman to take on these tasks. My father, being the youngest of five siblings, took over the family's winemaking business at seventeen years old. To this day, I believe he was robbed of the chance to figure out what he really wanted to do with his life.

My mother, raised in a strict Catholic household, was in the first year of women to attend the mathematical science high school. While academically gifted, she never felt she truly belonged on earth at this time. She was so spiritually connected and yearning for a world of love, peace, and a higher level of consciousness.

They both came from very modest families, and together, they built the wine business into an incredible and very successful company while raising three young children. While in business, they were an extremely creative team. Their romantic relationship looked different. I never felt that they were very loving, caring, or affectionate with each other.

My father was always filled with love. However, emotionally and physically, closeness did not come as naturally to him, and as a child, you yearn for that. My mother, coming from a very intense upbringing herself and still carrying unresolved stories, was way ahead of her time and did everything she could to raise us with as much love and consciousness as possible. She made us aware that there is much more to life than what meets the eye.

At a very young age, I felt I could achieve anything I set my mind and heart to, but I was under no pressure to do anything specific. I recall life force flowing through every cell of my being, with my heart wide open. One thing my mother always told me, and I even recall, is that I did not have judgment towards anyone. I would approach anyone and, to my parents' detriment and amusement, sometimes even invite them into our house for a meal.

You would think I had the best possible foundation.

And I believe I did.

However, our environment was a stark contrast. Our extended family, the school we attended, and most of my friends' parents held a different view of life, more in line with societal norms. This disparity slowly eroded my self-worth, bit by bit. Step by step, it began to rub off on me and took away my self-belief.

At eight, an unexpected event occurred that significantly diminished my self-regard. It was likely something completely different from what you might imagine.

We went on a holiday to Africa, specifically Kenya—Mombasa. I still recall this moment like yesterday. When we arrived in Africa, immense heat and humidity greeted me in a way I had never experienced before. We made our way to the shuttle bus that would bring us to our all-inclusive hotel.

I was sitting by the window, and my heart dropped on our way to the accommodation. I saw a level of poverty I had never seen before. We drove through one slum, and there was this little boy my age, maybe even younger, and he was so skinny, truly just skin and bones. He sat on the ground with two sticks and a plastic tarp above him for shelter. The bus came to a stop for a moment. The little boy looked into my eyes and gave me a thumbs down.

We then proceeded to drive into our fancy accommodation, which was filled with luxury, a stark contrast to the poverty I had just seen. Something happened inside of me on that drive. I was torn between the comfort of my surroundings and the suffering I had just witnessed. Nothing made sense anymore.

How could the world be so unfair?

How is it possible that I get to be here and this little boy was suffering so much?

It was the first time I experienced guilt for all that I had and the life that I lived. Feeling ashamed, I did not know how to deal with this at such a young age nor how to express what was going on inside of me. I felt part of my self-worth being ripped out of my chest. This trip changed something within me, and from that point on, a part of my self-esteem was gone and replaced with shame and guilt.

During my youth, I was very rebellious, and looking back, it was no surprise that the shame and guilt I felt turned into anger and, in moments, even rage. Anger toward myself but also anger towards the system, our society, and that we did not equally take care of our people.

Not being taught what a loving relationship looks like, I started dating my "first love" and moved to another city with him at sixteen. That turned bad quickly; he became emotionally and physically abusive. He also never worked and lived off my money, leaving me struggling. It was not until it got so out of hand that I feared for my life that I got the courage to leave him. In hindsight, it was no surprise that I chose that kind of man as my first boyfriend.

I did not feel worthy, so I chose someone who treated me that way. But I knew I would not let that happen again. Internally, I decided I wasn't going to let any man get emotionally close to me. I did not want to get hurt again.

I moved into an apartment. I was studying therapeutic movement and dance full-time, and in my spare time, I was taking extra dance lessons. Dance was my outlet, and I absolutely loved it. I was working at one of the coolest nightclubs in the city, behind the bar. While swallowing all the pain down and being very disconnected from myself, I loved my life. I felt free; he wasn't there anymore. I loved my studies, had amazing friends, and would often party. I was doing so much, way too much, but I had so much fun at the same time. From time to time, I injured myself, as my body needed a break and I wouldn't give it one.

This was also the time I met my next boyfriend, who, between us, never made me feel genuinely wanted, desired, or worthy. How could he? I didn't value myself. But he was much nicer than the previous one. I felt I was for sure upgrading. While living in Switzerland, we moved to New Zealand together. I knew what I wanted to do; all that was on my mind was dance, and I dreamed of opening my own dance school.

With financial help from my father and after endless back-and-forth with my ex, he decided he wanted to open a restaurant. So that's what we did. We opened a dance school and an Italian restaurant. Starting from scratch, we bought the land and built an entirely new two-story building. The plan was that I would run the dance school, and he would run the restaurant.

Oh, how naïve we were. I was twenty-one years old and did not have the slightest clue what I was getting myself into.

Within no time, the dream turned into a huge nightmare.

I was just running the dance school, and even though it was very successful, it didn't last. He was overwhelmed with the restaurant, and so much money came into it from my family. I ended up teaching dance and then working in the restaurant at night.

I was burning the candle on both ends. Our relationship was only about work, and we couldn't really stand each other anymore. Everything was too much until it came to the point of explosion. We broke up, and because most of the finances came from my family, he left me to keep it all going.

My oldest brother, who is also a chef, once told me, "Piera, if you ever need me, I am always here." He was living in Switzerland. I called him and said, "I need you. I need a head chef and a business partner, ideally yesterday." He dropped everything and was instantly on a plane. I will forever be grateful to him for doing that, and I will never forget it. What an absolute legend. While running the businesses with him was much better than with my ex, I felt so stuck. I was stuck in a life I did not truly enjoy. I never wanted a restaurant, and it took over everything. I was miserable.

And now we are back where I started this chapter.

I made a promise to myself: "I will make a change right now."

I found the first glimpse of my self-esteem and realized nothing was more important than my self-worth. No one else will make the change for me. No one else can. What an aha moment for me. It finally clicked. Repeating to myself: "No one else can. I am in charge of my happiness. I am the creator of my reality and have much more power than I think."

So, my journey of reclaiming and remembering my worth began.

And so it did.

Once I decided this internally, I was surprised at how easily the solutions to the dilemma I thought I was caught in began to appear. It didn't happen overnight, but within a relatively short time, everything untangled itself. We sold the restaurant, found an excellent lease for the building, and the dance studio kept going with other teachers.

I was finally free.

I needed a break and did not even want to think about the future, so I took a summer off, allowing myself to be a beach bum and investing more time into deepening my love for my yoga practice.

That summer, a massive 7.8-magnitude earthquake struck my small town, shaking us all to the core and isolating our little community for months. This meant that many of my friends unwillingly also got a few extra months off, and we just enjoyed spending time at the beach surfing, which was my new hobby. Just being together, I finally felt like I could relax.

I spent a few months deepening my yoga practice on Nusa Lembongan, a small island in Indonesia.

What happened during that time was more than I could ever imagine. It was the start of my understanding of how to love myself, regain my self-esteem, and remember the self-worth I was born with while also understanding the true meaning of yoga, which is self-inquiry and learning to calm the fluctuations of the mind.

From the moment I arrived on this little island, I instantly felt at home. There was something magical happening there. While it was a very quiet place, especially compared to Bali, the people seemed to be genuinely happy, kind, and loving. Life seemed to be much simpler, and no one seemed to care about your status or what you possessed.

All the teachers in my yoga training seemed like absolute goddesses. I was in pure admiration of the authenticity, peace, and love they radiated. They just seemed to live their best lives, fully in touch and embracing their emotions, while being in a place of gratitude for life. And soon, I understood why.

Every meditation I undertook, and every exercise of self-inquiry I delved into, brought me closer to my essence, sparking a joyous journey of self-discovery. I reflected on my life without judgment and understood why I made the decisions I did and what life brought to me. But way beyond that, I started to really like myself again. I felt this love inside of me I hadn't felt for a very long time. This love is present no matter the other circumstances; I was born with it. Like a suppressed memory, it just came floating back.

This love made me experience my worth again and truly feel cared for and taken care of by the universe. For me, this could only happen by finding stillness, spending hours and hours just breathing, and observing without judgment. And through the loving help and guidance of those around me who have already gone on this journey before me.

I observed a completely different way of life. I met the most beautiful people who quickly turned into lifelong friends. These people encouraged, uplifted, and celebrated each other, elevating our collective self-esteem.

I wanted to live this way, and there was no going back.

So I decided. Not knowing how, but I would keep studying and learning. I would move to this island and do precisely what these teachers did for me and others.

Going back to New Zealand was difficult. While I was already a confident yoga asana (the movement part of yoga) teacher, I now dedicated all my time to studying the ancient scriptures of yoga, diving deep into the philosophy of yoga that was so eye-opening for me, and taking so much time for meditation and self-inquiry. I make sure I fill my time with as much fun as possible, doing the things that uplift me and fill my cup. I stopped saying yes to all social events out of fear of missing out, stopped caring about what others thought about me, and instead focused on what I thought about myself.

A year later, I returned to Nusa Lembongan to study further. As soon as my feet touched the warm, sandy beach, I instantly felt at home again and knew I was getting closer to making this my permanent base.

While sitting on the beach on a full moon night, the moon reflected on the calm ocean before me, shimmering in full beauty with the gentle sound of the waves landing on shore. I wrote my clear vision: "In the next half a year, I am moving to this very island. I will teach at this school, which I adore, and live near my good friend. All of this will effortlessly fall into place through divine action. So it shall be." As I sat there, I could already feel how I was going to feel living here.

Six months later, I made the move I had envisioned on that full moon night. I had the job I wanted, was humble and full of love, passing on the tools I learned to regain my self-esteem. I moved next to my good friend and made this little island paradise my home. Also, within a few weeks, the cutest, skinniest, beaten-up puppy adopted me. He became my roommate and is still by my side to this day.

The journey of regaining and remembering my self-worth was not a journey that happened overnight. Instead, over the years, I gradually released all the layers I put on myself and, day by day, got to know myself more while using the tools I had gained to calm my mind and treat myself with kindness. I am still on this journey. At times, I still catch myself being judgmental or harsh towards myself, setting high expectations, and putting undue pressure on myself.

But guess what?

I know how to catch myself, and in every moment I do so, I don't judge but give myself a loving hug and change my limiting beliefs and outdated patterns one after the other.

I was opening my heart again and releasing all the wounds from my past relationships and experiences. I had promised myself that the next man I would be in a relationship with would be the kindest, most loving, and most compassionate man I would ever meet.

I vowed that my worth and happiness would always be my priority. I also understood that only by looking after myself and making sure my joy, love, and holistic well-being were number one could I be in a relationship where I could genuinely experience unconditional love. I wanted to be with a man who would prioritize his happiness, so we could come together and blossom, enriching each other's lives.

Once more, I declared this to the universe, and two days later, I met him. He embodies exactly everything I just mentioned. We met during the pandemic in a magically aligned situation that would take another chapter to write about.

We were enjoying the time and space to get to know each other and enjoy life on our quiet island paradise. We were falling deeply in love with each other. Because I now had my self-worth, I had attracted a man who treated me like a queen, and still does. Through this, I am enriching my life and changing an ancestral pattern of unhappy relationships that runs through the feminine line of my family. Almost four years later, we decided it was time for us to leave Indonesia and start a new adventure.

We are now back in New Zealand. Amongst our other projects, we started a YouTube channel—the Piera Maria Conscious Living channel—where I continue to share all the wisdom and tools that have changed my life. My deepest desire is to spread this knowledge and these tools to as many as possible. What better way to do this than to stream them for free?

We are getting ready to start a new chapter in life, and we couldn't be happier or more excited to welcome our first child into this world in a few months. This wonderful soul from the new time, who chose us as parents, is growing in my womb as I write this and is already so loved, wanted, and cherished.

While the eight-year-old version of me could not see how we could make this world a better place, the now 35-year-old version of me sure can.

I firmly believe that each of us, one person at a time, holds the power to make this world a better place. We are the change that the world is yearning for. By upgrading our consciousness through loving self-awareness, living our self-esteem, knowing our self-worth, and treating ourselves with kindness and compassion, we radiate that energy and affect others.

A shift is happening in this world. More and more people are coming to this same realization. Let's all start changing our society to uplift each other, genuinely celebrate one another, and come into greater harmony, not just with ourselves but with this incredible planet we get to live on. Let us be the generation that makes the shift, the generation that knows how to listen to our intuition and our inner guidance system. Let's be supported by our angels, guides, and helpers from the spiritual realm. Let's make lasting changes for the generations to come.

One of my most significant, enriching, and lovingly challenging tasks in this life is beginning now.

Together with my loving partner and our conscious community, we are committed to raising our children and future generations so that they never lose sight of their self-esteem and truly understand their self-worth.

They will have to learn their own stories and lessons. Contrast exists simply for the sake of our own growth. But I hope our children do not have to go through the same lessons in the same way we had to.

With every fiber of my being, I believe we can be the change we wish to see. I am committed to being a part of this movement, and I hope you will join me. Thank you for reading these pages. I hope that some of my words have touched your heart and given you the trust that no matter where you are in your life right now, you have the loving power to turn your life around, regain your self-esteem, and start living your best life.

"The journey to self-esteem is not linear—it's layered with learning, unlearning, and becoming."

— Unknown

Unlocking the Power of Soul Alignment

—◦◦◦◦—

By Lisa Duckworth

Have you ever looked in the mirror and wondered, "Who am I, and how did I get here?"

This simple yet profound question accelerated my journey of self-discovery. It's a question that guided me to look beyond the surface and into the depths of who I truly am. For years, I chased external validation. I was a stylist behind the chair, pouring my energy into making others look and feel their best. During those countless hours of conversations, I listened attentively as clients shared their struggles. Many spoke of having difficulty sticking to an exercise routine, winding down at night, or even getting a good night's sleep. These struggles, no matter how small or large they appear to be, often compound over time, deeply affecting one's self-esteem and overall well-being.

Difficulty with exercise routines can lead to feelings of inadequacy or frustration, while sleep challenges create a cycle of fatigue that affects emotional regulation and mental clarity. As a wellness expert, I understand how these barriers can feel insurmountable, but I also know how intentional strategies like creating structured routines, prioritizing self-care, and adopting mindfulness practices can break these cycles and pave the way toward a healthier, more confident self. They lamented their challenges with skin issues and their confusion about how to fuel their bodies properly. Their stories were strikingly familiar, mirroring my own hidden struggles. Over time, I began noticing that what were once vibrant tales of adventure and joy had transformed into narratives of stress, illness, and fatigue. I realized I wasn't truly living; I was merely existing.

This discovery set me on a path of change that would shape not only my life but also the lives of those I now coach. It's a story of rediscovery, resilience, and pursuing alignment with my soul's purpose. Along the way, I fell in love with biohacking, age-reversal techniques, and cutting-edge technologies that support optimal health. But most importantly, I found my self-esteem, and with it, the power to live authentically.

Movement as a Lifeline

Movement has always been more than exercise for me, it's a lifeline. As a young girl, I found freedom in dance. The music, the rhythm, the way my body moved, it felt like a language of its own, one that helped me process emotions too big for words. I can still remember twirling in my living room, feeling an inexplicable connection to myself and the world around me.

Years later, when life felt overwhelming, that connection to movement saved me again. I discovered ballet-inspired barre classes, which re-inspired my love for dance. Barre wasn't just about elegance and flexibility; it introduced me to strength and resilience. It became a sanctuary, a space to rediscover who I was. It taught me that my body could be a source of power and healing even in the face of adversity.

Movement wasn't just about exercise; it was my therapy and a cornerstone of my age-reversal philosophy. Practices like yoga and barre are more than physical activities; they are rejuvenating rituals that tap into the body's innate ability to heal and regenerate. Yoga, for example, combines breathwork with movement to lower cortisol levels and improve flexibility, both essential for reducing the cumulative impact of daily stress on the body, and simultaneously elevating one's self-worth. Barre, with its focus on posture and core strength, activates deep muscle groups, promoting long-term mobility and resilience. These practices also enhance mitochondrial function, the energy centers of our cells, contributing to improved vitality and slowing the cellular aging process.

They've been a lifeline, reminding me that every purposeful movement is a declaration of self-care to live into self-esteem. Engaging in purposeful physical activity doesn't just tone muscles or improve flexibility; it activates a cascade of benefits that promote longevity and youthful vitality. Studies have shown that regular movement reduces inflammation, increases mitochondrial function, and boosts endorphins, all contributing to age reversal. For me, movement became a way to reconnect with my inner self, proving that age is just a number when you prioritize your body's innate ability to rejuvenate.

On the hardest days, I turned to movement not for the physical benefits but for the emotional release. A brisk walk or impromptu dance session wasn't just an activity; it was therapy.

Through movement, I found reminders of my strength and glimpses of hope that carried me through dark times. Each step reminded me of the resilience we all carry within us.

The Dark Days: Rebuilding from the Ground Up

There was a time when I hit rock bottom. Divorce and the weight of life's uncertainties left me questioning my worth. I felt stuck, unable to see a path forward. But even in those darkest days, I found an anchor in movement. Although I had practiced yoga years ago, I rediscovered it through a different perspective during my difficult relationship and subsequent divorce. Yoga became my way to ground myself and dig deep, releasing trapped emotions. It allowed me to hone into myself on a deeper level, providing the stability I needed when everything else felt chaotic and uncertain.

As I began to feel the benefits of consistent movement, my mindset shifted. I felt lighter, not just physically but emotionally. That sense of accomplishment, however small, gave me a glimmer of hope. The movement reminded me of who I was and what I could become. It sparked a renewed determination within me to rebuild, not just for myself, but for my daughter, who needed a role model.

To rebuild my self-esteem, I also incorporated actionable steps like practicing positive self-talk, setting small, achievable goals, and confronting fears and uncertainties. I started by listing one thing I appreciated about myself each day, even if it felt uncomfortable at first. Over time, these affirmations planted seeds of confidence. Visualization also became a powerful tool, imagining the life I wanted to create and feeling the emotions of achieving it. Neuroscience supports this practice, showing how visualization strengthens neural pathways associated with success and resilience.

Journaling became another vital part of my healing process. I didn't write about calories or workouts, but about my emotions and the root causes of my pain. I explored what triggered feelings of self-doubt or inadequacy, and through this practice, I uncovered patterns and released emotional baggage. Over time, I integrated gratitude into my journaling, acknowledging the small victories that marked my progress. This shift in focus from lack to abundance was life-changing. It taught me to celebrate myself, no matter how imperfect my journey.

These small, consistent actions helped lay a stronger foundation for self-worth and growth. Each day was a reminder that even the smallest steps could lead to transformative change.

The Importance of Celebrating Your Wins

There was a time in my life when I diligently pursued my goals without celebrating my achievements. Growing up, I didn't clearly understand the importance of recognizing my wins. I would check off tasks quietly, believing that simply doing what needed to be done was enough.

This constant drive left me feeling like I was never doing enough, and I often overlooked the progress I had made. It wasn't until I began to consciously celebrate even my smallest wins, whether it was completing a challenging task, sticking to a healthy habit, or simply taking time for self-care, that I discovered the power of reinforcement. Each small celebration became a building block, revealing how these little accomplishments added up to significant progress. As I embraced this practice, I found myself more open to taking on new challenges and achieving greater successes.

Celebrating my wins not only boosted my self-esteem but also sparked a newfound motivation within me. Now, I encourage everyone to honor their achievements, no matter how minor they may seem, as they are the essential foundations of a fulfilling and empowered life.

The Power of Small Steps in Developing Healthy Habits

Creating healthy habits one step at a time is not just a journey; it's a transformative process that can profoundly change your life. As a wellness expert, I have witnessed firsthand how the path to self-esteem and well-being begins with small, manageable actions. Starting small is crucial because it allows you to build confidence and success incrementally. When you set an ambitious goal, it can often feel overwhelming, leading to frustration and discouragement. However, by breaking these goals down into bite-sized steps, you can celebrate each small victory, reinforcing your belief in your ability to change. One of my favorite things to say is, "Slow and steady wins the race." For instance, instead of committing to a rigorous workout, consider starting with a ten-minute walk each day. This act not only improves physical health but also boosts your mood and self-belief. Over time, these tiny changes accumulate, creating a ripple effect that enhances your overall lifestyle.

Moreover, these incremental steps guide you to your soul's alignment. When you engage in practices that resonate with your true self, whether it's through mindful eating, daily gratitude, or nurturing relationships, you connect with a deeper purpose. Each small habit you cultivate becomes a stepping stone toward clarity and fulfillment, allowing you to align your daily actions with your core values and passions. As you honor these small commitments, you create a life that feels authentic and meaningful, paving the way for profound personal growth. You see yourself as someone capable of making positive choices, and this shift is the bedrock of lasting self-esteem.

Ultimately, it's consistent, small efforts that lay the foundation for sustainable growth and fulfillment, bringing you closer to your true essence. Embrace the power of small steps, and watch as they lead you toward the life you've always envisioned, one that resonates with your soul's purpose and activates your inner light.

The Power of Transformative Coaching

Through my work as a wellness coach, I've had the privilege of guiding countless individuals on their journeys to reclaim confidence and strength. One client stands out in particular. A woman came to me feeling defeated by her struggles with weight and self-esteem. Together, we crafted a personalized plan that combined healthy food options, an exercise routine, and journaling techniques to address her emotional barriers. We also integrated age-reversal technology into her regimen, enhancing her vitality and well-being. Over time, she not only achieved her weight-loss goals, but she rediscovered her confidence and sense of self-worth. Seeing her transformation was a profound reminder of why I do this work.

Coaching is about more than providing strategies; it's about holding space for someone's growth, celebrating their wins, and empowering them to believe in their potential. The transformations I've witnessed are a testament to the power of intentional guidance and the strength of the human spirit.

The Path to Empowerment

Building self-esteem is a deeply personal process, but it can be guided. My journey has taught me the value of mentorship, education, and community. By sharing my knowledge, I aim to empower others to take control of their health and live to their highest potential.

It starts with small, deliberate steps. Begin by setting intentions that align with your values.

Prioritize self-care, not as an indulgence, but as a necessity. Surround yourself with supportive people who uplift and inspire you. Most importantly, trust the process. Growth takes time, but the rewards are immeasurable.

From Barre to Broader Horizons

Even before my divorce, I had embraced movement as a career. I was already a barre and fitness instructor, sharing my love of exercise with others. But it was after the divorce, when I found my passions reigniting, that I dove deeper. I became a certified personal trainer and nutritionist, fueled by a renewed sense of purpose. The more I immersed myself in these disciplines, the more I realized the profound impact they could have, not just on the body, but on the mind and soul.

Barre had given me a foundation, but my curiosity pushed me further. I explored strength training, yoga, and other modalities emphasizing both physical and mental wellness. Each certification and new skill was a step toward building a holistic wellness brand that could empower others to reclaim their health and confidence. These experiences reinforced my belief that true wellness is a harmonious blend of movement, nutrition, and mindset.

Nourishment for the Mind, Body, and Spirit

My journey didn't stop at movement. I noticed that what I fueled my body with had a profound impact on how I felt. Gone were the days of restrictive diets and chasing fleeting trends. Instead, I embraced whole, nutrient-dense foods that supported both my physical and mental health

As a nutritionist, I've seen firsthand how food can be transformative. It's not about deprivation; it's about abundance. It's about choosing foods that nourish your body, feed your mind, and uplift your spirit. Research highlights the role of anti-inflammatory foods like leafy greens, berries, and omega-3-rich fish in promoting cellular health and slowing aging. For me, it was a shift from punishment to love, from viewing food as an enemy to seeing it as an ally in my journey toward self-esteem.

Nutrition became a way to honor my body. I began experimenting with foods that made me feel energized and clear-headed. I discovered the joy of preparing meals that weren't just fuel but acts of self-care. I found a special joy in juicing, crafting vibrant blends filled with colors that seemed to radiate life itself. Cucumbers, beets, lemons, and apples became my palette, each glass a masterpiece of nutrients that energized my days. Smoothies became another passion of mine—fruit-rich creations featuring frozen bananas, berries, pineapples, and nutrient-packed additions like protein, sea moss, and burdock root that not only support detoxification but promote glowing skin and improved digestion. Each smoothie was not only delicious but a vibrant celebration of health and vitality. This mindset shift was empowering. It taught me that wellness starts from within and that the choices we make at the table ripple into every aspect of our lives.

The Mind-Body-Spirit Connection

One of the most profound lessons I've learned is that self-esteem isn't just a mental game, it's holistic. The mind, body, and spirit are deeply interconnected, and neglecting one affects the others. When I committed to nurturing all three, I began to experience true transformation.

Meditation and mindfulness became daily practices. At first, sitting still with my thoughts felt impossible. But over time, I learned to embrace the stillness, to listen to my inner voice instead of drowning it out with distractions. Those moments of introspection were pivotal. They allowed me to identify limiting beliefs and replace them with affirmations of self-worth.

Through yoga, I discovered a profound sense of connection. The movements were meditative, a dance between strength and surrender. Yoga taught me to appreciate my body for what it could do, not just how it looked. It became a practice of gratitude, a way to honor the vessel that carries me through life.

I also became acutely aware of the impact of what I allowed into my mind. I started by being intentional about the media I consumed, choosing podcasts, audiobooks, and videos that inspired growth and positivity. My mornings began with motivational talks or guided meditations to set a focused tone for the day. I limited exposure to negative news and social media that didn't serve my well-being. Instead, I curated playlists filled with uplifting music and affirmations that reinforced self-worth and resilience.

These small but deliberate choices created a mental environment where my mindset could thrive and align with my wellness goals. The content I consumed, whether through media, music, or conversations, had a direct effect on my well-being. I began curating what I listened to and watched, ensuring that it aligned with my values and supported my growth. This conscious effort to protect my mental space was just as important as nourishing my body.

Lessons in Alignment and Mentorship

One of the most valuable lessons I've learned on this journey is the importance of aligning with the right coach or mentor. Early in my entrepreneurial path, I found myself working with a business coach who, though skilled, wasn't the right fit for me. The misalignment led to overwhelm, burnout, and financial losses that felt devastating at the time. But in hindsight, it was one of the most transformative lessons of my life. It taught me the importance of trusting my instincts and walking away from what doesn't feel right, even when it's difficult.

Finding the right mentor is about alignment. It's about connecting with someone who not only understands your goals but also resonates with your values and vision. This alignment creates a space for growth and collaboration, where you can be guided without losing sight of your authenticity. However, being coachable is equally important. To be truly guided, you must be ready to make changes, embrace discomfort, and commit to the work required to achieve your goals. Growth requires effort, and the best mentors help you see possibilities you may not have imagined for yourself.

From Passion to Purpose

As I pieced together the fragments of my self-esteem, I realized that my journey could inspire others. My love for movement, nutrition, and mindfulness naturally evolved into a calling. I became a barre instructor, then a fitness instructor, and eventually a certified personal trainer.

Each step deepened my understanding of the human body and its incredible potential.

But I didn't stop there. My curiosity about age reversal led me to explore bio hacking and innovative wellness practices. I was fascinated by how small, intentional changes could yield profound results, not just in how we look, but in how we feel and function. Age reversal, to me, isn't about denying the years; it's about embracing vitality and living fully at every stage of life.

Starting my wellness brand, LuMarie Wellness, was a natural extension of this passion. I wanted to create a space where others could experience the same breakthroughs I had. Whether it's helping someone reset their fitness routine, refine their nutrition, explore age-reversal strategies, or even take the bold step of starting their own wellness business, my mission is to empower others to reclaim their health, self-esteem, and potential.

Investing in Oneself: The Catalyst for Growth

One of the most transformative lessons I've learned is the power of investing in oneself. I remember the pivotal moment when I enrolled in a comprehensive wellness program. At the time, I was hesitant, questioning whether I had the time, the resources, or even the capability to take on such a challenge. But deep down, I knew that investing in my growth was the key to unlocking a future aligned with my purpose. That decision not only expanded my knowledge and ignited a profound sense of confidence. It reminded me that taking risks for the sake of personal development is not a luxury; it's a necessity for true transformation. When I first began my journey, I was filled with self-doubt. Could I build something meaningful?

Would people trust me to guide them on their wellness journeys? The fear was real, but so was the desire to grow.

Through this investment, I unlocked opportunities I never thought possible. I immersed myself in cutting-edge education, learning from the best in the industry. I adopted a growth mindset, viewing each challenge not as a setback but as a stepping stone. This shift allowed me to embrace risks, step out of my comfort zone, and build the foundation of my wellness brand.

Investing in myself wasn't just a decision; it was the best decision I've ever made. It taught me that true growth comes from within. I took the leap and trusted that the effort would pay off. Today, I can look back with gratitude for the lessons learned and the self-belief gained.

Key Takeaways

1. **Movement is Medicine:** Purposeful movement heals and transforms, promoting youthful vitality and resilience. Practices like yoga and barre support age reversal and emotional well-being. Find an activity that resonates with you and commit to it regularly.

2. **Nourish Holistically:** Embrace whole, nutrient-dense foods and vibrant creations like juicing to fuel your body and mind, fostering sustainable health and cellular rejuvenation.

3. **Mind-Body-Spirit Connection:** True self-esteem emerges from nurturing all aspects of yourself. Incorporate mindfulness, yoga, and curating positive mental inputs to support holistic well-being and longevity.

4. **Celebrate Small Wins:** Acknowledge and celebrate progress, no matter how small. Each step forward builds momentum and reinforces self-worth.

5. **Vulnerability is Strength:** Sharing your struggles connects you to others and fosters growth. Embrace your imperfections as a bridge to meaningful relationships and self-acceptance.

6. **Invest in Yourself:** Investing in your education, health, and mindset is a catalyst for personal and professional growth. It's the key to unlocking your potential and achieving lasting transformation. Whether it's through personalized coaching, exploring age-reversal strategies, or starting your

own wellness business, investing in yourself paves the way for empowerment and enduring self-worth.

7. **Adopt a Growth Mindset:** Embrace challenges as opportunities for growth, and trust that each step, no matter how small, contributes to your journey of self-discovery and empowerment.

8. **Power of Small Steps:** Small, consistent efforts lead to transformative growth. Focus on manageable actions to build confidence, align with your purpose, and activate lasting change.

9. **Mentorship and Community:** Surround yourself with supportive mentors and a like-minded community. These connections provide guidance, inspiration, and accountability as you navigate your wellness and self-esteem journey.

Conclusion

Imagine waking up every day feeling energized, confident, and aligned with your soul's purpose. If you're ready to take the first step toward reclaiming your self-esteem, I invite you to join me on this journey. As someone who has walked this path, I am here to guide you with personalized coaching and support. Together, we can create a plan that aligns with your unique goals and empowers you to live your best life.

Whether you're looking to optimize your health, build healthy habits, explore age reversal, or even start your own wellness business, I'm here to help you succeed. Let's work together to unlock your potential and create a life that reflects your worth. Reach out to me today and take the first step toward living into your self-esteem. That's the power of self-esteem. It's not a destination; it's a journey, a beautiful, transformative process that starts with one courageous step.

Through movement, mindfulness, and nourishment, I've rediscovered my self-esteem and crafted a life filled with purpose and fulfillment. Launching LuMarie Wellness wasn't just a professional accomplishment; it was a testament to the power of perseverance and self-belief. It stands as proof that conquering fear and self-doubt can pave the way for unparalleled growth and empowerment.

If you're ready to begin your own journey of transformation, I invite you to take the first step. Whether you're looking to improve your health, rediscover your self-esteem, or align with your purpose, I'm here to guide you. Together, we can unlock the potential within you and create a life of vitality, passion, and fulfillment.

"Self-esteem is the reputation we acquire with ourselves."

— Nathaniel Branden

Seasons of My Self-Esteem

---◦◦◦◦◦◦---

By Liz Pembroke

I n my experience, our self-esteem can be a complex and
confusing subject that affects every area of our lives. Self-
esteem is how we value, perceive and respect ourselves and is based
on our opinions and beliefs about ourselves. With healthy self-
esteem we believe we are neither more nor less than one another,
unlike low self-esteem which makes us feel inadequate, or an
inflated/false self-esteem, which can make us feel superior. In my
experience, both come from a place of not feeling good enough.

I didn't used to have a tremendous sense of compassion for a
younger, insecure me, but in the past thirty years, I have learned
powerful life lessons, had amazing therapists, teachers and mentors
and have grown by listening to and reading other people's stories of
transformation, from feeling insecure about themselves to genuinely
living in a place of a healthy, fulfilling self-esteem. These
experiences have inspired me on my journey.

It is from that place of finally feeling at home in myself that I can
now reflect on my early years. I grew up as the eldest daughter of
parents who had been married for five years and wanted children. I
recall playing outside with friends in the quiet cul-de-sac of open
countryside where we lived. It was idyllic in so many ways, but
although I wouldn't have been able to articulate it then, I sensed I
was different from my other family members. I was sensitive, shy
and emotional, but my sister and parents didn't seem to be.

I remember being a very young girl of possibly only ten years old when boys started giving me a lot of attention, and I misinterpreted this attention as the love that I craved from my parents. It made me feel seen for who I was and valued in a way I hadn't experienced before. It was intoxicating. Yet the craving for that love and attention never seemed enough to satisfy the void in my heart.

At that time, I felt like a chameleon. I believed I needed to please people, as I thought it made people like me and protected me from rejection. I can see my self-esteem was more and more based on what I thought other people thought of me. At this time in my life, I really related to the Charles Cooley quote, "I am not who you think I am; I am not who I think I am; I am who I think you think I am."

I had many relationships leading into my late teens driven by the need to fill that void, to the extent that I would change my behavior to please the man in an effort to gain his love. I didn't feel like I had a choice in a relationship. I was looking for a sense of love, but not from a place of knowing and valuing myself. I was looking for a man to give me that value. I found men to be emotionally unavailable, but this pattern was likely driven by my unconscious desire to replicate that familiar feeling from my relationship with my dad; a relationship where I felt he wasn't emotionally available to me, which led me to create a feeling of resentment towards him.

I now recognize that I was looking externally to mask the pain within of not feeling good enough about myself, and appreciate the fundamental and legitimate importance, to healthy self-esteem, of being seen, valued and loved by my dad. So much research shows, and it's been my experience with all my clients over the years that a father's influence in his daughter's life shapes her self-esteem, self-image, confidence and how she views her relationship with men. Linda Neilson, a professor of psychology and expert in the field of father-daughter relationships, explains that an emotionally absent father can have a damaging effect on his daughter's life:

"When women don't grow up affirmed and acknowledged by their fathers, they can suffer from low self-esteem and make bad choices in their lives, often leading to an anxious attachment style, living in a state of fear and distrust."
— Neilson L, (June 2020) Improving Father-Daughter Relationships: A Guide for Women & their Dads.

My parents came from a generation, brought up during wartime, where loving emotions weren't openly expressed, so they weren't equipped to express love in the way I needed. I now know that they absolutely loved me to the best of their ability, and this is not about blaming them in any way. This is only an understanding of why I never felt good enough. At sixteen, I fell pregnant and had my first abortion without telling my parents. I was very naïve and believed it was just going to be a medical procedure. I did not realize how it would affect me, nor in particular how much further it would deflate my self-esteem and increase my sense of shame.

Nevertheless, I continued to repeat the pattern of seeking what I believed to be love, resulting in two more abortions into my late twenties. These experiences compounded my feeling of not being good enough, the senses of shame and self-loathing and being a victim to my circumstances. I didn't ask for help until I had therapy later in my life. I stuffed the emotions of guilt and shame away.

After leaving college, I worked in the corporate world until, at 29, I met my husband-to-be. He was a charismatic, successful entrepreneur, twenty years my senior. He owned several businesses, which gave me a sense of security and safety, giving me false self-esteem. We married and I immediately found myself in the role of stepmum to five children, as he had a number of previous marriages. However, early in my marriage, I realized I did not really know my husband. He was not only emotionally unavailable, but also became very unkind in his behavior, physically and mentally. Had my self-esteem been more robust and healthy, I would not have accepted this. I felt ill-equipped to deal with the unkind behavior, other than to continue to try and make it okay at the expense of my own well-being, not realizing I could say no.

The transformative experience of being in therapy myself, combined with a spiritual awakening propelled me to become a therapist and join and train with a transformational organization. This brought a huge sense of worth, firstly from that deep sense that I was loved, then finding an area of life where I felt excited to my core, learning about healing modalities for mind, body, soul and spirit. I learned that celebrating each step of progress to be hugely helpful in building my self-confidence, rather than focusing on perfection and always feeling I fell short.

I can now embrace more fully when I fail, as just part of the important growth process, not that I'm a failure. I have experienced that as I continue to accept, love and nurture all parts of me, actively growing into being my most authentic self, my self-esteem inevitably grows in tandem.

I always had a deep longing to have children but had convinced myself it wouldn't happen because of the shame I felt following the aborted pregnancies. However, I was exhilarated when I fell

pregnant in our first year of marriage, but this feeling was short
lived as I suffered a traumatic miscarriage. I felt this loss was my
fault, again not feeling good enough. It was a further two years
before I fell pregnant again, and again after another four years, with
the birth of my two girls. When I held them for the first time, I felt
an indescribable depth of love. They were the most beautiful
experiences of my life. They changed my life, lifting my self-esteem
and reshaping how I see myself and my purpose in life.

However, the challenges persisted in my marriage and alcohol
became something I relied on to numb the pain. My aunt introduced
me to the twelve-step program Alcoholics Anonymous (AA), which
gave me a renewed sense of feeling seen and welcomed. This was a
community of people who spoke honestly about their experiences
and feelings with no judgement. It was a scary experience going to
my first meeting, but I can see how overcoming my fear of reaching
out and asking for help allowed my self-esteem to grow. Meeting so
many people who were on the journey of valuing and loving
themselves and who offered to let me join them was life-changing.
At the same time, it was painful to face my vulnerabilities and to do
this was totally unfamiliar to me.

I had spent most of my life looking for other people's permission
for who I should be and what I should do, never feeling I could get
it right, but this process enabled me to understand that by self-
reflection and taking radical responsibility for how my life was, was
very empowering. A whole new sense of confidence and self-esteem
was now opening up, as I gradually saw how my brutally unkind
words towards myself were not really true. I had no idea that I was
speaking to myself so harshly or the detrimental effect that was
having on me.

It was during this time that I experienced another transformative moment in my life. There were still times when I felt distinct lack of purpose. I recall sitting on my sofa and feeling a certain hardness in my heart and I asked God to 'show me his heart for people.' It wasn't long after that in answer to my prayer that I had an overwhelming compassion for prisoners and a desire to make a difference in the lives of those needing support in prisons. It seemed like everywhere I looked, every newspaper or TV program was about prisoners. This was an area of life I had never thought of before. I had not known anyone who had been to prison and knew nothing about the prison system, so I felt totally out of my depth with zero knowledge or experience. Because the prison world was so alien to me and was taking me way out of my comfort zone, I knew it must be a true calling from a power beyond me. I had to be resourceful to find my way into prison. Everyone I spoke to thought it was a bad idea and advised me against it. I continued to follow the compassion I felt and did eventually become a volunteer with a number of charity organizations that ran faith-based courses and restorative justice programs throughout the UK. I could share how I was learning to value myself and how transformative knowing I was loved by God was. It made me realize even more, how much, those of us who act out in seemingly unloving and destructive ways, just need loving and guided on the journey of self-esteem, the most.

This experience taught me that the space outside my comfort zone is where I grew in confidence the most. I had previously thought that I had to wait until I felt confidence to do anything, but I now know that I first need to be still enough to hear the quiet voice of my intuition, trust it and take action. In doing so, my confidence and self-esteem naturally rise because of achieving something new.

I learned a lot from my time in prison, particularly about the power of forgiveness. The raw, stripped-down nature of prison life left no room for pretense, offering a safe space to share my story with inmates who were eager to understand and reflect on their own lives. One of my most treasured memories is receiving a painted bookmark from an inmate, expressing gratitude for simply being heard and telling me that it helped him avoid suicide. I've experienced breaking free from a sense of shame through the healing power of being truly heard, whether in prison, with friends, or a therapist. As Andrei Lankov said, "To not have your suffering recognized is an almost unbearable form of violence," emphasizing the emotional toll on our self-esteem of not feeling we can honestly share our painful experiences versus the freedom of having our true story heard.

Spending years in high security prisons with men who had committed heinous crimes helped me see beyond their actions to their inherent worth. Everyone is born with the potential for healthy self-esteem, but that can be damaged in hostile or neglectful environments, affecting behavior in negative ways. I saw that guilt, when reflected on, could lead to positive change, whereas shame, which makes us feel inherently wrong, only deepens self-doubt. Offering unconditional love and support in prison allowed me to witness its transformative effect on many inmates' self-worth. It's those who act out the most who need love the most, as it's through this unconditional love that healing and restoration of self-esteem happens.

It was during my time volunteering in prisons that I felt the calling to become ordained! "Really God, you want me to become a vicar?" I did pursue this route formerly, but realized that it actually meant finding a role that suited me in my unique expression of sharing the love of God. I eventually led an organization that ran retreats for church and business leaders. As a leader, it can often feel isolating, so having a safe space to talk openly about what's going on internally was an incredibly powerful experience during the retreats. Being alongside peers who are going through the same challenges made it even more meaningful, a reminder that we're not alone in facing these struggles. I was also involved in other community building ventures, focused on the marginalized in society.

Then at fifty-three years of age, my life took me in a completely different direction again. We had been together for twenty-five years when my husband decided to end our marriage. Up until this point, my husband and I had built an outwardly very successful life in terms of a business and a beautiful home we had designed and built ourselves that backed onto open countryside. It all fell apart when I was hit with the shock that my husband was having an affair and was not being honest in our relationship. We had to sell our home. I lost my family life as I knew it and it had major financial implications. I had lost everything, including my physical and emotional wellbeing.

By the time he left, my self-esteem was at ground zero again, and I experienced a breakdown in all areas of my life. I was physically unable to eat and lost about two stone. I barely had the energy to get up in the morning and mentally, it felt like my mind had stopped working. Except, that is, for its ability to generate very self-critical thoughts. Emotionally, I was numb except to crippling anxiety and depression. It had been a gradual process, like a frog that starts in warm water that gradually heats up, until the frog is unwittingly boiled alive.

I honestly felt like I had a sticker saying "stupid" on my forehead, which produced a deep sense of shame. One of the hardest things for me during this time was trying to be the best mum I could be while knowing I was failing miserably. I remember a song that used to play in my head: "*I Love You Just the Way You Are*" by Barry White. I was grateful for that small glimmer, even though it felt like it was coming from a distant place.

I had no choice at this point other than to rely on my community of friends. My stepdaughter set up a rotation of friends and my amazing church community did the same. They brought food each day, mostly soup, and they would just sit with me, as it was too much to talk. The healing this brought to my sense of self-esteem is invaluable. I had to let go of my sense of worth being about what I could do for everyone else and accept help just for me.

It was during this time of hardship that both of my parents passed away. They both passed in the space of just three years. They had been married for over sixty years, and were my consistent solid ground, and wonderfully supportive grandparents to my girls and stepchildren. My dad was honest to the core of his bones and exuded integrity in all he did. My mum was kind and strong, and always supporting others. I had the privilege of having them in my life for fifty-four years. It was a shocking loss to me, one that took me years to navigate. Eventually, I came to an acceptance that this is a natural part of what it is to be human.

My mum was in a hospice for the last two weeks of her life. On the day she died, I was working and suddenly, I knew I had to be with her. I left work and was by her side, holding her hand, when she passed away within the hour. It was such a privilege to be with her.

I was so grateful I trusted my intuition, and acted on it, something I hadn't always done. That experience helped me lean into knowing I can trust the internal guidance that had been there all along.

One incident that had an unexpected accelerating effect on my self-esteem was when my dad went into hospital for a straightforward heart valve replacement. The operation didn't go to plan and he ended up in intensive care. The moment I saw my dad, who had once been a strong, tall man, in that hospital bed, unconscious and helpless, I experienced a deep sense of love and compassion for him that instantly eradicated any lingering resentment I had held against him. It was instant forgiveness for him and for myself.

One day when I was in hospital with my dad, I had the feeling I wanted to tell him I loved him. This seemed to take a lot of courage as I had never said this to him before, as I was always hoping he would say it to me. Yet on this road of forgiveness, I took responsibility for what I wanted and told him I loved him for the first time (I was now in my fifties!) and to my absolute delight he responded with "I love you, Lizzie." My heart felt like it was going to explode and I walked out of the hospital ten feet taller. It made such a profound difference to how I felt about myself. I had the wonderful yet painful privilege of being the one holding my dad's hand when he passed. The gift of that experience was profound. All that felt important in that moment was my love for him and the gratitude I had for him as my dad.

I continue on my journey of nurturing a healthy, robust self-esteem grounded in My personal value system, not what I think I "should" or "ought" to have to be "successful," something I would now call false self-esteem. I look at life as a huge garden to explore. I have come to realize we are not all excited by the same part of the garden. I only have to nurture and dig the part the garden that excites me. I don't have to dig the whole garden, or critically compare my part to others. I reflect on the very dark times in my life and I am now grateful for them, seeing them as nourishment in the soil of the garden of my life that has encouraged new growth in me.

I have grown through my experiences and I understand the truth of Franklin D. Roosevelt's words, "a smooth sea never made a great sailor." I had erroneously learned to avoid the painful storms of life rather than facing them and embracing them as a part of what it is to be human. The tough times have forced me into trusting God, learning the power of sharing my vulnerability, asking for help, forgiving others and myself and accepting life has a natural order, just like nature. Seasons change, and that's okay; we aren't meant to stay in summer all year long. In the learning of new skills, step by step, my self-esteem expanded.

I believe we are born knowing in our deepest soul that we are unconditionally loved and with our self-esteem fully intact, ready to flourish. Like an apple seed, we have everything inside us to grow into a flourishing apple tree, but then life happens! I learned to make sense of the world from a very early age by telling myself I was stupid, not good enough, not pretty enough, not safe to be seen as my true self. My life was on the rails of thoughts and beliefs I'd created as a young girl, which I believed at the time to be true. As I worked hard at changing those false self-critical thoughts to loving thoughts towards myself, my self-esteem is so much more robust. I'm now looking for my authentic value from within, not from comparison-based self-criticism.

The building of my self-esteem is an ongoing process, one that isn't linear, but I am not swayed by the extreme lows of critical self-talk or the artificial highs of judging my external performance. In my last thirty years as a therapist, counselor, mentor, life coach and spiritual seeker, and having lived the different seasons of my own self-esteem, there is one verifiable truth with everyone I have encountered. Whether they are in prison for the rest of their life or living free as royalty, when we feel loved for who we are, not for what we do, we all flourish and find deep inner peace with ourselves and others.

Through educating myself and continually seeking teachers and people that lovingly but strongly reflect to me what I don't know about myself, I have gained clarity on my behavior, my self-critical mindset, their root causes and the consequences for my self-esteem. Through the process of forgiving others and myself, changing my mindset and continuing to flex the muscle of becoming more self-aware, I have integrated with compassion who I was at the different stages of my life, as a child, adolescent, mum and step-mum. This has increased my self-acceptance, self-respect and self-esteem.

As Michelangelo famously said when asked about how he carved his statue of David from a single block of marble, "I just removed everything that is Not David." So it has been with me, a gentle chipping away (sometimes a more painful hacking) of what is not authentically me. It has taken courage and I had to learn to slow down and be present with myself and observe the beauty and simplicity of nature. It knows just what to do and I learned it's no different for us.

I like to keep it simple. Explore who you are, get to know who you are, love who you are and enjoy being at home with who you are in your unique expression. Remember who you are at your core! Peace, love and joy are the fuel that allows us to have the most full and nourishing experience of life. I like to think of us all as a human orchestra. Every one of us has a unique expression, each instrument as valuable as the other, adding to the complete unity of all life.

There is so much healing power in having our stories of struggles heard. It would be more commonplace if we hadn't created society in such an individualistic way, where we have lost the sense of being and belonging in community. I'm very grateful for you reading and hearing mine.

"The most powerful relationship you will ever have is the relationship with yourself."

— Diane Von Furstenberg

The Bridge to Fulfillment

By Matthew White

I once read a quote that said "nothing is real; it is all perception." I look at my journey today and I think back to where I was just ten years ago... and the perception I have of myself compared to now is so big I almost don't recognize the person I was before...

Sometimes I joke on stage when I'm speaking to crowds and a photo comes up of me twelve years ago and I refer to him as "Bob, the construction worker." This guy Bob had no self-esteem and no confidence, other than he was a hard worker.

Today helps transform lives... gives people new beginnings and takes people on a journey of self-discovery and success in business and life where they can make an impact speaking on stage...

If you asked Bob whether this would be possible, he would simply stare you down and tell you to F... off.

Life is merely perception... what you tell yourself and how you act is the baseline of your life... It is the foundation of how people see you and I have learned it is the strength of your self-esteem.

The Ember That Wouldn't Die

As any entrepreneur knows, when you have a calling, it burns deep inside you, no matter what life hurls at you. That calling becomes a roaring fire of passion and purpose, and at its peak, you can practically hear it crackle. For me, that fire almost went out when a metaphorical tsunami of life's challenges doused me in a flood of self-doubt. But here's the thing about a flame that's meant to burn: it never really goes out. At worst, it shrinks down to a stubborn ember, just waiting for that spark to reignite it.

During some of the toughest years, that ember was little more than a whisper in my heart, repeating over and over: "You are called to serve… you are called to serve…" I tried to move on, bury myself in construction work, using it as an escape from the dreams that once burned within me, and forget my ambitions. But as time passed, I noticed that ember regaining strength, turning into a small flame, then a medium flame, surging every time I dared to dream again.

Then, of course, *impostor syndrome* and fear of failure would rain back down, threatening to snuff out that glimmer of hope. But it refused to go away. I felt trapped in a cycle of frustration: my self-esteem was tattered, and I questioned my identity, losing sight of who I really was. Something had to change. I couldn't keep trudging through life tied down by what I call "golden shackles": a decent paycheck but zero fulfillment.

I was working as a site manager, supervising the construction of multi-story apartment complexes and boutique developments, big projects often in the ballpark of 180 million dollars. I'd show up first thing in the morning, leave last, and coordinate a crew of about 40 people. By the end of each day, I'd be drowning in stress.

A Maserati and a Moment of Truth

Then came the lightning-bolt moment. One afternoon, a developer came onto the site. I had no idea who he was at first, but soon found out. We started chatting. Well, *he* did most of the chatting, and I did the listening. He bragged about all sorts of deals he had in place and, in particular, how much money he expected to pocket. He was tossing around numbers like confetti, but one figure hit me right in the gut: $7.8 million. That was his profit when all was said and done.

I'd been breaking my back for years, working harder than anyone on-site to make far less than what I knew I was worth. Meanwhile, this guy strolled off to his Maserati and roared away. My blood pressure soared. In that instant, a fire tore through my chest. It was anger and clarity all at once: I had been trading my time for money, building someone else's wealth while strangling my own dreams.

When I got home, I told my girlfriend about this encounter. Her reaction? A shrug and the comment, "Some people are just meant for bigger things," and in that moment, I felt a pang of doubt in my self-worth, wondering if I was destined for something greater. The implication, of course, was that I wasn't one of those chosen few. I barely slept that night, lying awake like a caffeinated chipmunk. I was angry; angry at myself for not doing more, and angry at the world for making it look so easy for people like him.

The Decision to Burn the Bridges

Morning came with heavy rain. My mind was darker than the storm clouds. I sat at the foot of my bed, tears rolling down my cheeks as the conflicting voices in my head did battle. One voice hissed, "You're not good enough. You'll fail. You're an impostor." The other demanded, "You are called! You can't ignore this forever!"

Despite my fear, I recognized I had to commit fully. I knew the only way out, *the only path to real freedom,* was to burn my bridges so thoroughly that I couldn't go back.

That day, stalled in rainy morning traffic, I took out my phone and snapped a picture of the sea of red brake lights in front of me. I said to myself, *"This is the moment. I will never forget it."* After that drive, I handed in my resignation at work, which kicked off a few of the hardest weeks of my life.

Impostor syndrome unleashed fresh torment:

"You're dumb. You're going to fail."

"Who's going to hire you?"

"You know nothing about the internet!"

Still, I planned my escape down to the last detail. I had to make sure there was no turning back. On my last day, I invited everyone, including colleagues, bosses, and subcontractors, to a farewell get-together. I bought a ridiculous amount of alcohol and basically torched every relationship I had there with unfiltered honesty. Fueled by booze and desperation, I unleashed years of pent-up frustration. Let's just say it wasn't my proudest moment. I stumbled away a drunken, bloodied mess, but I'd succeeded in slamming that door behind me. No going back.

The Entrepreneurial Restart

A strange calm settled in after that. It was the quiet before the storm. Yes, impostor syndrome roared back soon enough, whispering new lines like, *"You have no idea what you're doing,"* and *"Who would listen to you?"* But now, I had no fallback plan. My back was against the wall, and I had to move forward. This was also the moment I realized how critical self-esteem is when you set out to build something from scratch.

I threw myself into what I jokingly call my personal "Entrepreneur University," a school of hard knocks unlike any other, losing money on investments, facing rejection, and working late nights trying to make sense of it all. When I was younger, I'd never read a book cover to cover. I left school early, having zero formal education. I quickly learned that there was a wealth of information out there, and I intended to soak up every drop of it.

The Shiny Object Distraction

The internet, ironically, is both a fountain of knowledge and a fire hose of distractions. I learned about business strategies, marketing, real estate, coaching, and more. I would pivot to one idea, then pivot to the next, splashing around in every bright, shiny opportunity that popped up. It was maddening. My money was running out fast, and I still hadn't nailed down a plan.

Then I attended a real estate seminar where the speaker wrote on a board: F.O.C.U.S. = Follow One Course Until Successful.

She explained that fear of failure (sitting at the top of the line) will pull you off your path, while distractions (sitting at the bottom of the line) do their best to yank you down. The key is to stay on that straight path, the "bridge of fulfillment," and continually ask yourself what it will take to stay focused.

Her words were like a light from the heavens: I had no *clear* plan. My path was foggy, my "goals" basically a pile of scattered dreams.

Drawing the Bridge to Fulfillment

So the next morning, I grabbed a giant whiteboard, a prized possession. I drew a straight line from one side (where I was) to the other (where I wanted to be). At the top of the board, I scribbled "Fear of Failure," and at the bottom, I wrote "Distraction." The line in the middle was labeled "Bridge of Fulfillment."

Suddenly, it hit me: *I need actual steps.* I drew vertical lines along my bridge, labeling them Step 1, Step 2, Step 3… up to Step 21 (yes, 21!). Each step represented some practical action that would move me closer to my big goal: becoming a successful real estate coach. Naturally, *impostor syndrome* crept up again: *"Who do you think you are, anyway? You're just a construction guy!"*

As I slumped in my chair, I heard a little boy outside shouting to his brother, *"You can do it! You can do it!"* Somehow, that snapped me out of my funk. I marched up to my whiteboard and wrote: "You can do it… You are called." I realized *this* was the missing piece of my puzzle. It wasn't enough to just plan steps; I had to *believe* in my ability to achieve them.

This marked my first real taste of the power of self-esteem, that unshakeable belief in yourself. It was the fuel my internal fire needed. From then on, I started mentally reframing my question from "Can I do it?" to "What must I do to make it happen?"

A Mind and Body Makeover

With my new plan in place, I dove deeper. I realized self-esteem isn't something you flip on like a light switch; it's something you *fuel* constantly. And that fuel comes from knowledge, discipline, and consistency.

I also faced an inconvenient truth: I was overweight, roughly 25 kg (55 lbs) heavier than I wanted to be. My old beliefs about low-fat diets and healthy eating had led me astray. New research I stumbled upon indicated that your mindset is shaped by much more than just your brain; your whole body plays a part. Get your body healthier, and your mind follows suit.

So I drew another line on my whiteboard, my "Body Transformation Plan." I learned everything I could about nutrition, supplements, exercise, and sleep. I switched to a low-carb, high-fat regime, cut out junk, and scheduled workouts. Five months later, I was down from 114 kg to 94 kg and had abs for the first time in 30 years. I was more energized, more focused, and most importantly, my self-esteem rose to new heights.

The (Not-So-Easy) Path to Real Estate Coaching

My partner, Sahara, and I both had a passion for real estate. We started by purchasing properties and renting out rooms, turning them into positive cash flow opportunities. I struggled to break into the real estate coaching space at first. People didn't know me, and the competition was fierce. I went to countless seminars and spent entire nights with my nose in books or glued to YouTube, searching for that one breakthrough strategy.

Finally, I discovered a *hidden loophole* in real estate investing, one that could save people at least $80,000 on their properties while boosting their monthly cash flow. Once I tested and refined this loophole, word got out and suddenly people were reaching out, wanting to pay me for guidance.

Then came the big moment: a real estate guru invited me to speak on his stage. A part of me screamed, *"Are you insane?! You can't speak in front of a thousand people!"* But I said yes anyway, because I realized I needed to figure it out.

Facing the Stage Fright

Despite a zero on my public-speaking resume, I knew I had to seize this opportunity. I studied the techniques of famous speakers, watching YouTube clips until my eyes crossed. In *Think and Grow Rich*, Napoleon Hill talks about building an imaginary mastermind of people you admire. So I created a mental panel of top speakers and pretended they were coaching me.

I prepared my slides and story, then kept tweaking them until I drove myself (and Sahara) half-crazy. The night before, I barely slept. The morning of, I was a ball of nerves. I peeked from backstage at the sea of faces. My heart pounded like a jackhammer.

Then I remembered a trick I'd read about: I counted down from ten, my mind zeroing in on each number, pushing away the fear with every second that passed. Once I hit zero, I told my imaginary mentors, "Let's do this!" and walked onstage, pretending to be one of those confident speakers I'd studied.

Boom! The music started, and I launched into my talk. I had the crowd laughing, cheering, and taking notes. By the end, they were clapping. *Clapping!* for someone who, just months earlier, had been on a construction site cursing at developers in Maseratis. That moment changed the trajectory of my life and gave my self-esteem a rocket-powered boost.

Engineering My Days for Success

It was around that time I recognized just how vital structure and routine are to maintaining a high level of confidence. I realized I couldn't just wing it every day. I needed discipline that would protect me from old habits: distraction, procrastination, and the dreaded self-doubt.

So now, my days are crafted with the care and precision of a Swiss watch:

Early Rise: I'm up at 4:30 a.m. every day, no excuses.

Morning Meditation: A quick, focused 15-minute session sets the tone.

Exercise: Sahara gets up at 5:00 a.m., and by 5:15 we're both out for a workout—strength, cardio, or something gentle like yoga. We do it outside, rain or shine, without a gym to distract us. Over 2,000 consecutive days now!

Supplements: We follow a strict regimen to keep energy and focus up.

Deep Work: From 7:00 a.m. until noon, my calendar is blocked. No calls, no emails, no social media. I work in 90-minute bursts with short breaks to reset my mind.

Midday Break: Lunch is healthy, and I stop coffee at noon to avoid afternoon crashes.

Power Nap: A 15-minute doze on the couch right after lunch. When the timer goes off, I'm back at 100%.

Shutdown: By 6:00 p.m., the workday is over. Period. We eat dinner, read, and dim the lights. By 8:30 p.m., it's lights out so I can rinse and repeat.

I know it might sound extreme, but the structure frees me to be more creative and confident. Instead of feeling caged, I feel energized and clear-headed. There's no wasted time or mental bandwidth on "What should I do next?" It's the best system I've found to maintain high levels of self-esteem.

Investing in Knowledge (and Myself)

I'm a big believer in my grandfather's saying: "Knowledge is power." Over the years, I've invested over $330,000 in my education, from seminars and coaching to online programs. It's paid off by more than $24 million in sales. That's some serious ROI. But more than the money, it's the confidence that comes from *knowing* you have valuable skills to offer the world.

What people really pay for is *skill*, not just passion. Sure, passion is nice, but if you can't deliver results, you will not build a thriving business. So I kept sharpening my digital marketing expertise, learning how to run ads on social media platforms, launch e-mail campaigns, and create compelling offers. It was painful at first. I got banned from Facebook, lost money on misguided ad campaigns, and questioned my sanity more than once. But eventually it clicked, and clients started pouring in.

One-to-Many Selling: The Stage Beckons

When my one-on-one schedule maxed out, I realized I needed to transition to "one-to-many" selling. I organized my small meetup event, half-convinced no one would show. But to my surprise, 42 people attended. I told my story, explained my system, and at the end of that session, over $300,000 in coaching packages sold. That's the beauty of speaking from the stage. In a single talk, you can touch so many people and compress weeks of one-on-one calls into a single evening.

The Real Magic of Self-Esteem

My journey from losing everything to regaining my entrepreneurial spark wasn't easy. My self-esteem tanked so hard at one point, I wondered if I even deserved a second chance. But I've learned that self-esteem is the golden key to every entrepreneurial door. You can have the best funnel in the world, the greatest product, and the biggest ad budget, but if you don't believe in yourself, you'll sabotage the whole thing.

Conversely, self-esteem isn't just blind confidence. It's nurtured by *knowledge*, *practice*, and *results*. You need to do the work, physically, mentally, emotionally, and stack small wins until you trust your instincts.

These days, I'm still obsessed with pushing myself. Despite having achieved more than I ever imagined, I keep my back close to the wall, constantly taking steps forward so I don't stagnate. That flame inside me roars louder than ever because I feed it daily with action, discipline, and the occasional pep talk: *"You can do it... You are called!"*

Parting Thoughts: F.O.C.U.S. is Wealth

In the end, I've learned that what you focus on is what you get. Self-esteem is what allows you to focus with clarity and drive. The life you want really can be a straight line, as that seminar speaker demonstrated. Plot your path, label your steps, and figure out how you'll overcome the fear and distractions clamoring to pull you off course. Don't be afraid to burn your bridges if that's what it takes. Sure, the voices of doubt will never fully disappear, but with a clear mission and unshakable self-esteem, you can take on any challenge that comes your way.

So ask yourself:

- Where do I want to be?

- What steps do I need to take to get there?

- How will I drown out the noise trying to stop me?

Then, make it happen. Because you *can* do it. And if you ever doubt yourself, just imagine a kid in the distance yelling, "You can do it!" Trust me, it works.

Remember: Self-esteem is the fuel. Focus is the engine. Together, they'll drive you anywhere you want to go. Let your ember roar, and before you know it, you'll be burning brightly, lighting the path for yourself and everyone who's lucky enough to come across your fire.

"If you want to improve your self-worth, stop giving other people the calculator."

— Tim Fargo

How I Lost Myself, Found My Soul, and Became a Quantum Empath

∞◦◖◗◦∞

By Rebecca Sarr

The Moment I Lost Myself

We lay in bed together, with the afternoon sunlight dancing through the window and onto our tangled sheets. It didn't feel like a breakup moment, as our skin spoke embodied truths that denied the words that were to come.

Sam exhaled slowly. His eyes became distant. He said, "I don't want this anymore."

I had just returned from overseas, and we had been apart for months. The letters we had shared while I was away had felt so deep. So intimate. So pure. And so loving. I had been anticipating our reunion with the type of fierceness that only *true love* can provide. As far as I was concerned, Sam was my soulmate.

All the evidence was there. We *felt* each other. Even over thousands of kilometers of distance, our hearts felt connected, intertwined as one. At least, it had felt that way to me. And perhaps, over the great distance that had made my heart so fond of his, I had forgotten the hard and sticky parts of our relationship. The struggles, the tears. The confusion and the miscommunications.

While apart, it was easy to dream up the perfect romance. Now, back together, we faced an inevitable truth, one that he covered with a lie that shattered my heart to pieces.

"You're a sad person. And I don't want to feel responsible for that."

The shattering was slow. These words hit me quietly, not like a bullet or a blow. They seeped into my sense of self-esteem, like the poison of Snow White's apple, as she fell into a deep sleep.

My sense of self slowly broke apart.

My mind processed the words themselves. *I'm not sad, though...am I?* Instances of my childhood flashed before my eyes. All the times I had been brought to tears, not understanding why, simply being overwhelmed with emotions that I couldn't express.

And the words that would come next:

"Why are you crying?"

"What's wrong?"

"You're too sensitive."

I could never answer. I could never explain. There just weren't enough words to express how much I was seeing, understanding, and feeling in those moments. How every little word, action, movement, and look would spark up a chain of lightbulbs that interlinked with each other in the universe of my own mind, like a spider web of cognition that kept spinning forever.

And when it all felt so overwhelming and impossible to share, my body would take the reins to settle my poor mind's confusion. It would express itself beyond my control, simply through hot pinpricks of cooling tears.

The only words I knew how to say when someone asked me the inevitable, *"What's wrong?"* were, *"I don't know."* And so I guess that could appear as a kind of sadness for some?

Even so, but for my partner to label me as a *"sad person"*? It felt more than just painful. Sam was someone I believed truly understood me. He was the person I trusted most in the world. I thought back to all the happy times we'd shared, this young 'love of my life' and I. We had laughed and danced and held each other so tightly over the years. The joy I'd felt in those moments seemed incomparable.

And so his words had a power over me. They invalidated my entire inner experience, reducing the complexity of my senses and emotions into a single, dismissive judgment.

I could feel my self-esteem fracturing, tearing itself apart. While Sam's words broke my heart, they also planted a doubt in my mind that began to grow. Maybe he was right; maybe my inner world wasn't valid or worthy of understanding. This erosion of self-trust felt slow yet relentless. It made me question the truth of who I was while gradually dismantling the foundation of my own worthiness.

My sense of self-worth and self-esteem would fight against itself as realizations and insights about who I really was moved through:

I'm not sad. I feel every emotion more than others. The intensity of my inner world doesn't discriminate. I feel joy at holy levels. When I dance, it's like I'm touching divinity itself. When I love, I love to the depths of the other's soul and we intertwine as one. And when I cry, the tears flow like flooding rivers to the sea. There's no holding back. My body is free.

Something inside me kept speaking, holding up the possibility that my experiences were valid, that I was worthy of being understood in all of my beautiful complexity.

What I didn't know at the time was that I didn't just feel emotions; I absorbed them. People's words, their energies, their unspoken truths all entered me as if they were my own. I didn't only sense what others felt, I became their feelings, drowning in waves of sorrow, joy, or anger that weren't even mine to hold.

And Sam? I was realizing that I had allowed his presence to become the most intoxicating of all. I had lovingly welcomed his energy as it wrapped around me and washed through me, as it pulled me deeper into a soul-to-soul entanglement I couldn't explain. I thought this was true love. I thought this was normal for people who'd found their soulmate.

And so Sam's words that night, *"You're a sad person,"* completely annihilated me. They shattered my confidence in who I was and in everything I had believed to be true. It was not just because of the words themselves but because of the dissonance between what Sam had said and what I knew. While his voice told one story, his energy shared something else entirely. His lips denied what his soul whispered to my heart, and the contradictions shattered me.

The Lies I Believed

At just 23, I didn't yet know that I was an *empath*. It would take another seven years before I even encountered the word. Before that, I didn't have any language to describe how I was different; no box to place myself or my experiences into. And in fact, it wasn't just a case of empathic overwhelm in the way most people think of it today. It wasn't just empathy that I was experiencing; I was becoming consumed by a telepathic tether I didn't understand or know how to control.

When Sam walked away, the connection didn't break. If anything, it grew stronger. The heartbreak he refused to acknowledge lived inside me as though it were my own. It wasn't just about *feeling* Sam's energy. I could *hear* it. Even as we drifted apart physically, our spiritual connection only grew more intense. I remember those times so vividly when it felt like I was at the edge of what it meant to be alive. I would curl up in bed and listen to his voice around me, as his soul told me so many things that would never dance as words spoken directly from his lips.

Entire conversations unfolded silently, and Sam's deepest truths whispered themselves to me, even while he denied them. I had become an open channel, and I had no idea how to control it. And without control, it was overwhelming. I was constantly bombarded with noise. It was maddening. Sam wasn't even there, and yet his thoughts, emotions, longing, and regret would hit me like a tidal wave crashing on the shore: words that weren't mine, emotions that surged through me without warning, and insights I didn't always want to receive. I struggled to separate *me* from *him*, and the deeper my telepathic connection became, the more exhausted I felt. I was drowning in a constant flood of Sam's thoughts, emotions, and soul-level transmissions.

Was I imagining it? Had I truly lost my grip on reality?

Whenever we saw each other, I would mistakenly try to compel Sam to admit what I was hearing. I would respond to the unspoken questions he asked me, or challenge him on his lack of integrity in my presence. In response, I would be met with wide eyes and nervous laughter. Or even worse, anger, invalidation, and complete denial.

As I let the slow shattering of my heart break my self-esteem to pieces, I became terrified that I would be labeled as not only sad but schizophrenic.

"I'm crazy. I must be crazy... Am I crazy?"

Were the constant noise and overwhelming emotions symptoms of my own instability?

If he was not *The One* who completed me, and I was not actually hearing the wholeness of his soul speak to my broken heart, there could be only one other possibility.

Sam's words would echo in my mind as I did everything I could to quieten the noise and act normal. I convinced myself there was a part of me that really *might* be crazy, or that I was making it all up. It felt easier, at times, to believe that none of it was real. That I was just a sad person, and he had moved on.

And, believing what I had to in order to survive, I began to block out my intuitive abilities. I ignored the messages. I convinced myself I was overthinking. I let the lie that I was a sad person permeate my world, contradicting the truth for which I had no compass. Little by little, I shut it all down, allowing the poison of those four simple words to silence the power of my soul, to cut myself off from the very thing that made me *me*.

With nowhere else to place the pain, I retreated into books and busyness, hoping structure would replace sorrow. I surrounded myself with new conversations, new causes, anything to drown out Sam's voice in my heart. Whenever I was around those who knew us both, I couldn't stop the tears. The depth of my heartbreak was inconsolable, and nobody understood what I was actually going through. How could they? A group of budding law students in our early twenties, none of us had any framework for understanding empathy and telepathy at all, let alone at the confronting intensity that I was experiencing the phenomena.

I had no idea, back then, that the tears on my cheeks weren't proof of some kind of defective *sadness* in me. I was ignorant to the fact that the tears, instead, indicated the brilliant capacity I have to embody the deepest feelings at the highest levels. I had no idea that my unacknowledged abilities to sense emotional shifts in a room, hear unspoken words, and hold space for emotions that weren't mine were not part of some grand flaw in my design, but a gift that could help heal the world. My shattered self-esteem wouldn't allow it.

And so, I drew further and further away from him and all of our friends, in an effort to get myself back together, to find some sense of self again. Over the course of four years, Sam and I had formed a tight-knit circle around us, and it wasn't easy to undo the stitches.

His friends were now mine, and mine were now his. Moreover, it seemed as though no one cared to help me carry my own heart, which at the time felt like such a heavy cross to bear. So he and our friends carried on, with the parties, the drinking, and the drugs. They invited his new girlfriend to play with them, as I disappeared from their view more and more.

I thought I was healing. I thought I was growing stronger. But in reality, I was retreating into a version of myself that was quieter, smaller, and easier to digest. A version of me that wouldn't make anyone uncomfortable. A version of me that didn't threaten the structure of reality I had been given.

I didn't realize it then, but denying my gift and allowing myself to believe I was sad (and maybe even crazy) was wounding me more deeply than anything else. And my journey back to self-esteem wouldn't be about proving I was worthy of anyone's love or approval. It would be about reclaiming the empathic and telepathic power I believed, at that time, was my curse.

My Journey of Unlearning and Reclaiming

I did what I could to cut off all contact from Sam and our friends. I buried myself in my studies and turned my vision outward toward the rest of the world. As a fourth-year law student, it was easy to occupy myself at university. As I began to talk to new people and delve into more of what university life offered, I found a renewed inspiration in human rights and social justice.

Eventually, I stopped hearing Sam's voice everywhere. I stopped hearing our friends' voices too. No longer did I imagine conversations where I stood up for myself and told them how they'd hurt me. I buried what I could. I closed down the parts of myself that I couldn't understand, those parts that nobody else wanted to.

What I know now, as I come to love and honor myself more and more, is that with every death comes a rebirth. Shutting down my gifts wasn't just a wounding, it was a recalibration. A necessary breaking apart so something new could emerge. I didn't realize it then, but my higher self was already guiding me. Every choice I made, every step I took away from the old world I had clung to, was preparing me for something far greater than I could comprehend.

As I processed the pain of losing my fairytale, a voice that seemed to come from beyond me, and yet from deep within, made the promise: "*I will never have another selfish love again.*"

It wasn't just a promise; it was a declaration. An agreement between the small, wounded self I was still nursing and the power of my soul that was calling me forward. It wasn't just about letting go of notions of a white wedding and happily-ever-after. Looking back now, I see so clearly that it was about stepping into a love so vast, so boundless, that it had nothing to do with the human need for validation. And in surrendering the chase for such validation, I discovered the kind of self-love that would heal my sense of self-esteem from the inside out.

Rooted in wholeness rather than need, it was love that wasn't about taking, but giving. It was the love that would one day pour through me, and not deplete me but expand me, empowering me to reclaim my worth, rebuild my self-esteem, and finally stand fully in the truth of who I am.

I didn't know it at the time, but this was the beginning of my initiation. The moment I unknowingly began the long journey from overwhelmed empath to the founder of Quantum Empathy Technique (QET), a powerful healing, awakening, and co-creative modality that allows practitioners to tap into the power of the heart-space and translate the light of clients' souls, allowing for deep emotional, energetic, and spiritual shifts to unfold.

I began to meet so many new people and hear so many new stories that my awareness expanded in novel and exciting ways. Traveling overseas for a year before Sam and I broke up had given me a taste of how diverse life could be outside the comfort, safety, and conditioning of white, middle-class Australia. Seeing the limitless ways in which people lived, survived, and thrived in the world, from Hoi An to Paris, Wuhan to Quebec, Oaxaca to Tikal, freed me from so much programming around how I thought I *should* live, and where I thought I was failing.

For years, I had measured myself against invisible standards of who I should be, how I should act, and what kind of life I should want. But as I traveled and immersed myself in different cultures, I saw that life could be lived in a thousand different ways, none of them wrong. All of them valid. For the first time, I realized that the ideas of *success* and *happiness* I had been chasing weren't really mine. They had been given to me, handed down by a society that valued status over authenticity, achievement over alignment. And in that realization, something in me cracked open. This opening allowed my self-esteem to expand. I began to open my awareness to the possibility that I could forge my own path and not simply follow what society expected of me.

On coming home and being cast out of all I was familiar with through my breakup, I felt compelled to continue my quest of exploring different cultures and ways of being in the world. I volunteered, teaching English to people who'd arrived in Australia as refugees and asylum seekers. I began working with children from the Horn of Africa, and I traveled around Australia undertaking internships with organizations in remote Aboriginal communities. (I would eventually also work professionally as a criminal lawyer with the Aboriginal Legal Service.)

At the same time that my heart felt freed in these spaces, my eyes were opened to some of the harshest truths of humanity's existence, and this rocked me to my core. Coming to understand the inequality of the world also seemed to validate the pain I still held over the venomous words Sam had spoken to me.

"Of course I'm sad" I remember saying to myself one day. *"Look at what's actually happening in the world. Who wouldn't be?"*

What Sam never said is that, in his heart, he knew I was tiring of the privileged law student party scene we'd all been so caught up in. Looking back now, I understand what he was doing. He was protecting himself, projecting me as problematic so that he didn't have to feel his own feelings. And I took the bait, hook, line, and sinker because I didn't have the self-esteem to leave the situation of my own accord. I didn't have the confidence to say that it was all beginning to feel stale, that this was not who I was, and that I wanted something more. I didn't have the self-awareness at the time to realize that *this* was my deepest truth. And so I allowed myself to be scapegoated, to be wrong, and to be sad.

Reclaiming my self-esteem meant unlearning the lies I had believed about myself. The lie that feeling deeply was a flaw. That my ability to see and hear beyond spoken words was insanity. That my sensitivity was *too much*. I began to understand that being pushed out of the safety of my relationship and our friendship group, in the cruel way that I was, opened the doors for me to explore myself more fully. I began to build a new understanding of myself and the world around me. I began deeply reconnecting with my own truth.

As I did, over the years, my romantic space became filled with suitors who expanded my world, and my capacity for love expanded beyond the romantic in turn. As I began to embed my most meaningful relationships and friendships in cultures beyond the West, I began to encounter new ways of connecting and relating to other people and to the world.

I turned my heart toward Africa, both traveling around the continent and exploring African and Afro-diasporic cultures in Australia. I was shown love that was open, raw, vulnerable, and heart-centered. And I became familiar with ways of living that felt more at ease, more in flow, and more personally empowered than anything I'd known. These experiences gave my own heart permission to open itself up once more, in all its rawness, vulnerability, and power, not just in romance but in all aspects of my self-understanding, self-love, and self-esteem.

With every new experience that expanded my awareness, I felt an unraveling of the old conditioning that had kept me small. I didn't have to be this perfect lawyer-type with all the trappings that went along with it. I didn't have to fit into any kind of mold, whether it was one shaped by friends, family, or society at large. And I certainly didn't have to silence my heart just to make others more comfortable.

I realized that there was space in this world for my big, beautiful heart to shine as I saw the same light reflected in others. Little by little, my shattered sense of self began to rebuild and regenerate, transforming into something even greater than before.

From Knowing to Living My Highest Truth

It wasn't until almost two decades later that I fully embraced my empathic and telepathic nature. A series of profound mystical experiences, ranging from an intense, unbridled kundalini awakening to channeling unknown languages and receiving vivid messages from beyond the veil, left me with no choice but to realize that it was my life's purpose to share QET with the world.

QET isn't just about feeling energy; it is about speaking the language of the soul to guide people back to their truth through heart-to-heart telepathic connection. This unique part of myself, which I once saw as my deepest flaw, became the very source of my expanded sense of self-esteem. By embracing who I truly am, I transformed the shame of my sensitivity into the foundation of my strength, self-worth, and purpose.

Now, I feel blessed to work with my heightened sensitivities as I guide empathic souls back toward their own fullest sense of self-esteem, transforming what once felt like a burden into a profound source of empowerment, healing, and wholeness.

At first, when my Quantum Empathy re-activated, it felt scary to receive entire downloads of someone's soul story in an instant. With only a name, I could know someone's truth beneath the layers of conditioning. I could speak their pain, their purpose, their unexpressed emotions, and more. The responsibility felt overwhelming.

Who was I to hold this kind of power? Who was I to walk this path?

But every time I questioned my worth, the Universe would send me undeniable signs. Clients would experience enormous breakthroughs in mere moments. Synchronicities would guide my path. Miraculous healings would happen, and seemingly impossible transformations would be realized.

This was real. The feedback was undeniable and immediate.

I discovered that to share QET work with the world, my challenge would not be acquiring new skills or information. It would be growing fully into my self-esteem, with the understanding that my soul's path was so much bigger and so much greater than the human "I" could grasp.

It was about letting go of the ego-driven part of myself that wanted me to stay small. It was about accepting that my gifts weren't random, nor were they something to hide. QET was my calling, my soul's purpose. Every challenge I'd faced along this journey had supported me to live into the kind of self-esteem needed to share such powerful healing light with the world. The kind of awareness that understands: *I Am.*

And so, I began an enlightening process of refining my Quantum Empathy. Instead of resisting my abilities, I leaned in. I experimented, researched, and channeled until I had developed a clear, reproducible method that could be taught to others. I worked to become the embodiment of what I taught by living, breathing, and surrendering in trust to the power that was asking to come through me.

No more waiting for permission. No more fearing what others would think.

Quantum Empathy isn't something to be intellectualized. It is a power to allow one to activate from within.

To do so required a deep, unshakable trust in myself. A trust that when I open my mouth and allow myself to speak, the words coming through would shift energies, healing, awakening, transforming and co-creating. A trust that my heart is capable of holding space for the soul's deepest healing, and that I don't need to *do* anything except speak all I feel.

The more I surrendered and allowed my empathic feelings to be heard, the more powerful the work became. The more I allowed my heart to speak the language of the soul, the greater QET's impact on the world. The more I trusted that I was not, in fact, crazy, but a brilliant example of a gifted Quantum Empath, the more powerfully and beautifully my energetic mastery developed.

I've come to realize that true self-esteem means living and speaking your truth without hesitation, no matter how "out there" it may seem to others. For me, it meant owning my intuitive gifts without allowing others to make me wrong for how deeply I felt the world.

Now, through the Quantum Mastery Academy, I teach others how to master their own empathic and telepathic gifts through QET. I mentor overwhelmed empaths to shift into quantum mastery, and to "speak the field" with clarity, precision, presence, and power.

I truly believe that as more and more sensitive people rise into self-esteem, find their souls, and become Quantum Empaths, the world will become a more caring, compassionate, and connected place to be. When we honor our capacity for empathy, trust our own intuition, and allow deep presence to become a catalyst for real change, humanity's potential become limitless.

Through my journey as an empath living into self-esteem, I've learned that when we honor the truth of our being, we don't just heal ourselves. Our frequency ripples out into the collective, and the world heals together.

And, this is where I truly have found the light of my own soul. In the purpose of guiding others to rise into their soul's deepest truth, and activate Quantum Empathy within their hearts.

"The better you feel about yourself, the less you feel the need to show off."

— Robert Hand

Finding Self-Worth

—◦◦◦◦◦◦◦—

By John R. Spender

D o you remember that weird time when the world changed? Everything became more intense; new emotions rose from inside and…

Well, I wouldn't know if it was real love. It *felt* like it, but I'm pretty sure it was an infatuation. You know what it's like at that age: you watch him or her, wondering why your vision blurs, your heart beats faster, and you can't stop thinking about her. We've all been there.

The thing is, I didn't believe I was good enough to ask her out. I let self-doubt hold me back for months. But as summer break approached and the thought of not seeing her for weeks set in, something shifted. I realized that if I wanted to grow my self-worth, I had to take action, even if it scared me. So, with a little encouragement from my good friend Luke, I finally found the courage to ask Kristie out.

Her response?

"I don't like you. Your breath smells!"

It stung, sure, but strangely, I felt proud. Not because of her answer, but because I had taken the risk. Every time we act from a place of courage and self-respect, we strengthen our self-esteem, regardless of the outcome.

She had the tact of an angry bull, but then again, she was a kid herself. For many people, this may mean nothing, but to hear something so harsh, so early in life, when you felt something, even if it wasn't real (or "adult") love... it hurts.

I mean, had she simply said, "Sorry, you're a nice guy, but I don't feel the same," fine, maybe I could have gotten over it. But that sentence was like a blade through my heart, or more accurately, my entire chest.

These things are like stones thrown into the ocean. You see them sinking at first, but then they reach those dark depths, down, down into the abyss, and you don't even know that a rock is down there, deep in your gut, or rather, in your soul.

And the ripples it makes become a tsunami. But years later, you don't even know where it's coming from. You'll agree now that my fear was real.

Now I'm going to tell you how it grew. Like an unfriendly Neptune, it became the "god of my depths" inside of me, gnawing away at my life up there on the surface.

I spent the rest of my school years underperforming, not because I lacked intelligence, but because I didn't believe I had the right to take up space. It wasn't about missing out on becoming a rocket scientist or chasing the top grades. It was deeper than that. If I didn't understand something in class, I stayed silent. Not because I didn't care, but because a voice inside me, let's call it Neptune, kept whispering, "Don t ask. You ll just embarrass yourself."

That voice was fear, disguised as protection. But really, it was holding my self-esteem hostage. I was avoiding questions, and I was avoiding the chance to believe in myself.

Then, even thinking about another girl... For years I forgot about that strange feeling. It wasn't for me, or so I thought. But nature is nature, and I felt it again. But where could I find the courage to say those scary words again?

And yet again, my rule was: *"Shut up."*

What's more, those ripples were louder than thunder. Every time someone scolded me or I felt even slightly embarrassed, it felt as if my whole life was at stake, as if it had been questioned, criticized, and humiliated.

Even small things, like, "Why did you wear that silly hat?" left me speechless. I just felt deeply sick inside. And with time, this became my normal "way of being." It became who I thought I was, *myself.* Or so I thought...

I really wanted to continue doing drama; it was my favorite class in high school. But I didn't know how to pursue a career in acting. I struggled to articulate what I wanted. And I know why. It takes courage to "put yourself in the limelight," to show your skills and merits. As usual, I felt safer staying quiet, a wallflower looking upon life without ever being a real protagonist.

Throughout school, I always had a part-time job. I delivered papers and milk, and stocked shelves with groceries. Fine, we all have to start somewhere. Then I studied horticulture at a TAFE college, working part-time as a landscaper. I dedicated myself to learning. I was good at the theory but initially struggled with the practical side of things.

I had my comfort zone, and I took baby steps outside my little world. For me, it was fine. Or was it?

Let's say it was just that, *fine*. The comfort zone, I mean. But what about my life? No, it wasn't fine. It simply existed, and horticulture became my escape.

I don't mean to say that I was escaping, technically speaking. Maybe I was, maybe I wasn't. I never asked a psychologist. I mean it was like a never-ending avoidance, at least emotionally.

That's it! "A never-ending emotional escape!"

But you know what? Even though you're riding the wave of a tsunami, with Neptune controlling your life from the depths of the sea, there is still sun and wind outside. Other waves, even modest ones, will form and meet you along your path.

As you might expect, my closest friends reflected where I was with myself. We played it cool, skipping class, sneaking smokes behind the basketball courts, and being little troublemakers. But underneath the surface, a lot of it was just posturing.

My best friend, Jaime, was different. He carried himself with a kind of effortless confidence, especially around girls, and I secretly admired that. When we surfed or just hung out, I felt safe being myself. Over time, that environment helped me see myself differently. A bit of his self-assurance rubbed off on me in how I dressed, acted, and valued who I was.

Looking back, those moments were more than just typical teenage fun. They were early steps in learning how to live into my self-esteem.

Jamie helped me through my adolescence, and I think I helped him too. We were like two crutches supporting each other. Despite the forking paths of life, we've remained friends for many years. Only now, however, do I truly appreciate the importance of that friendship.

Many years later, I was struck by love again, like lightning, with nowhere to hide except in my safe zone.

Her name was Pauline, and there was a sweetness about her... like a flower, a peony. A peony, yes! Those charming blossoms that seem to say, "I cannot and will never harm you; I am safe." They're not as showy as orchids or roses. Best of all, they have no thorns and aren't demanding.

She changed my life. *"This time,"* I thought, *"I don't want my love to be silent, to have no words."* But as you know, the "guy downstairs" was telling me again that it was safer to shut up.

And now you'll ask me, "Where did you find the courage?" Here's the story...

I was at a fancy dress party with some friends when Wonder Woman approached me with a gentle smile. She was good-looking, fit, and confident. As Pauline came closer, she tripped over an extension cord, and I caught her drink over half my face. She blushed like a tomato and apologized profusely. I smiled.

"Accidents happen!" She laughed, and in that moment, I saw the light of the moon.

To make up for the awkward start, she invited me out for a coffee, and I mean actual coffee. That first meeting turned into many more, and within three months, Peony—oops, Pauline—and I had moved in together.

It was a turning point in our relationship and in how I saw myself. For the first time, I felt grounded. Loved. Valued. And that shift gave me the courage to believe in myself. I launched a small landscaping business around Sydney's eastern suburbs, something I had only dreamed of doing before.

With each new client and completed project, my confidence grew. I saw my worth in what I could do and what I could build. Within a year, I had a small team backing me. For the first time, I had the freedom and self-belief to take holidays and explore the world. Pauline and I caught the travel bug hard, hopping from country to country, chasing sunsets and new experiences.

But what I was really chasing, and slowly discovering, was my sense of self-worth. I was building a business and a relationship. I was building a life that reflected the belief that *I mattered.*

Diving deeper, this time into clear waters, I learned that if you don't love who you are, then that "you" is not really *you*, if you catch my drift. It's just a character, the one others want you to be or, more simply, the one others are used to. You please them by always giving the same performance to yourself and your audience. You've been typecast.

But that was the pivotal moment, the big change in my life. Of course, things are always changing, but I love myself, and when I look in the mirror, I can say, "Yes, this is you."

Finding love can feel like a powerful affirmation of our worth, but real growth often brings challenges that test our sense of self. When you're grounded in self-esteem, it's easier to navigate those challenges with clarity and compassion. My relationship with Pauline was full of love, but we were heading in different directions. She wanted children, while I felt called to continue the work/travel lifestyle.

It was a painful realization, especially because we truly cared for each other. She was four years older than I and had experienced deep loss, having lost a child in a previous relationship. Letting go wasn't easy, but honoring our paths became an act of self-respect.

I went to Madagascar for a month to reconnect with myself. She later married and had two children. Last I heard, they were still together. Choosing my truth wasn't easy: it was about a sense of freedom and exploration. The decision was ultimately about living a life aligned with my values.

I eventually sold my landscaping business and transitioned into Neuro-Linguistic Programming (NLP) coaching, public speaking, and writing. It was a huge leap outside my comfort zone, a real test of my self-esteem. My family thought I was crazy and tried to talk me out of it, but deep down, I knew it was the right path.

The year-long intensive NLP coaching training I took part in was both challenging and rewarding. I was surrounded by an amazing group of people, and the dynamic environment brought out the best in me.

Within a few years, I was living in Bali after completing a contract with a U.S. NLP training company based there, facilitating sessions in Singapore. With the support of a mentor, I launched a six-month online coaching program. She encouraged me to add a unique bonus for my clients: a book where each participant could share their personal story.

That idea sparked the birth of the *A Journey of Riches* series. Since then, we've published 40 books and collaborated with over 400 co-authors from 50 countries around the world.

All of us have put our fears in their place. Each author, little by little, gained confidence. The most amazing thing about all this is that we blossomed together. I can't tell you how beautiful it is to feel that there are many, many people like you, each with a story, each with fears, all learning how to raise our self-esteem.

It has been a magic carpet ride of a journey, true, and it's not over yet. But I feel it so strongly that each author will go on to bigger and better things. Yes, I have a certainty!

And again, this feeds back into my self-esteem. I can't say I'm soaring, but I'm flying now.

Which leads me to the other project I've been working on.

Sitting on the beach in Ungasan, Bali, I imagined a vision board in my mind's eye. I went home and created a real, tangible vision board that included all the people I found inspiring. Once complete, I kept staring at the people, places, and things I had placed on the board. It included people like Tony Robbins, Wayne Dyer, Jack Canfield, Dr. John Demartini, Michael Beckwith, Rhonda Byrne, and many others.

Looking into Rhonda's eyes, an idea sprang forth: I had to make a documentary film.

The thought of making a film terrified me. But the idea stuck and wouldn't leave me alone. My carry-around book at the time was *Think and Grow Rich* by Napoleon Hill. In one of the last few chapters, he talks about creating an imagery council of people who have inspired him, both present and past. Reading that chapter again, I intuitively knew what I needed to do next.

I sat in my bedroom with my vision board, inviting the various thought leaders to attend our first meeting. Tony Robbins was the first to arrive, with a direct yet sincere demeanor. Wayne Dyer was kind and respectful. One by one, all the leaders made their way to my imagery table with the agenda of discussing my documentary about the gift in adversity.

I have yet to meet a single person who hasn't experienced some form of hardship in their life. As such, I felt called to explore the concept of how your worst day in life can, over time, transform into an invaluable event, one that raises your self-esteem and shapes you into the person you are today. Often, a valuable vision unfolds gradually, with each step revealed in due course.

I don't recall how many imaginary after-work meetings I held. One of the loudest voices was Michael B. Beckwith, the spiritual maverick and founder of Agape. After a while, the conversations felt real in my mind, like telepathic communication.

I remember Michael saying to me, "I love the vision for the film. Let's make it happen."

I said, "How?"

"Come over to Agape and it'll all come together," he replied. "You'll see."

I know it sounds crazy, but it felt so real that I couldn't ignore it.

I booked a flight for myself and my videographer, Yoga. When we arrived in Los Angeles, a buddy of mine introduced me to his ex-girlfriend, who became our assistant. The plan was to act as if Michael had already said yes to being filmed.

We arrived early on Sunday, February 14th, 2016, at the Agape Spiritual Center in Culver City. We brought all our film equipment, intending to film him that day.

It was a little brisk, but there wasn't a cloud in the sky, and the sunlight was glowing on the pear blossoms in the parking lot. It was an inspiring scene, and Yoga started taking photos. Suddenly, I heard a loud voice shout, "What on earth do you think you are doing?"

A tall man dressed in white, with ginger-brown hair and a gold scarf wrapped around his neck, stormed over. Looking like a spiritual bodyguard, he made Yoga delete all the photos he had taken. With an English accent, he then turned to me and asked, "What are you doing here, and why don't you have media passes?"

I briefly explained the vision for the film. His expression immediately softened. He said we needed to chat with Jaclyn Brown and told us to follow him. The three of us exchanged smiles and followed him.

We waited at the main entrance while the spiritual bodyguard went inside to find Jaclyn. She came outside and greeted us with a smile, asking me about the documentary. I explained that it was about the gift of adversity and how good things can come from bad experiences. She beamed and said, "This is the paradigm that Agape was built on."

Jaclyn then said we needed to speak with Leaha Brown, shouting as she went to find her, "We are not related!" After chatting with Leaha, she organized VIP passes for us, and we sat in the front row for Michael's spiritual sermon. A week later, we filmed our interview with Michael.

At its core, you cultivate self-esteem not through external validation, but by honoring inner whispers, especially those that terrify you.

The fear I felt about making a film wasn't a sign to stop; it was a signal that something meaningful was calling me. Instead of backing away, I leaned in. I didn't know *how* it would happen, but I trusted the *why*. That single decision to say yes to my intuition was an act of self-respect. That's where self-esteem begins; in moments of private courage, when no one else is watching.

Imagination is not an escape, but an opportunity to prepare oneself for future blessings yet to be received. By gathering a council of mentors, real or imagined, you give yourself permission to be guided by wisdom greater than your current circumstances. That act alone demonstrates self-worth: the belief that your vision is worthy of counsel, support, and realization.

There will be confrontations, moments of awkward improvisation, and risks that could easily end in rejection. But if you have a vision rooted in truth, not ego, you'll be more likely to keep going. Every obstacle becomes a stepping stone. And slowly, reality meets your imagination halfway.

You forge self-esteem by honoring your inner voice, showing up when it's uncomfortable, and holding your ground, even when the outcome is uncertain.

In the end, self-esteem is not the loud confidence we display to others; it's the quiet trust we build with ourselves when we refuse to abandon our deeper calling.

Now, it doesn't matter whether you're making a documentary or simply finding your confidence in smaller, everyday moments. What truly matters is this: people with low self-esteem often share one common thread, the absence of belief and the hesitation to take meaningful action.

But here's the truth; when you challenge your doubts, when you value the quiet wisdom within you, and when you recognize that fear is only trying to keep you safe, not small, something shifts. Its voice no longer dominates. It softens.

Others may not understand what drives you, or why you're drawn to certain paths. That's okay. Let them drift by with their assumptions. It's helpful if you're willing to dive beneath the surface, to meet the part of yourself (call it your inner Neptune) that has allowed old fears and memories to shape your worth. Heal there. Begin there.

Remember, you are not weak. You are not "too much" or "not enough." You are beautifully sensitive. That sensitivity is not a flaw. It's your compass. Protect it. Honor it. It's part of what makes you powerful.

So why am I telling you this?

Because my fear begged me not to.

And I've learned that's exactly when I must speak.

**"To establish true self-esteem,
we must concentrate on our successes
and forget about the failures and
the negatives in our lives."**

— Denis Waitley

AUTHOR BIOGRAPHIES
Julie Blouin

Julie Blouin is a Certified Professional Coach and a leading voice in the personal development industry with over 20 years of experience. She has spent her life embodying the journey from personal mastery to powerful leadership, and demonstrating that true impact starts from within.

Julie is a 4-time international bestselling co-author and has written over 200 articles on career, health, and relationships. A recognized expert in empowerment, mindset, and business coaching, she has facilitated transformational courses and corporate training for hundreds of employees within organizations named among Canada's Top 100 Employers.

Beyond the corporate world, Julie is a trusted, results-driven coach devoted to lasting transformation. With authenticity and integrity at the core of her work, she empowers others to rise, lead, and create meaningful impact. She also helps purpose-driven individuals monetize their passions and turn their gifts into thriving, aligned businesses.

Soon, Julie will be featured in the powerful documentary *The Gift in Adversity*, alongside legendary figures such as Jack Canfield, Dr. John Demartini, Michael B. Beckwith, John R. Spender, and many more.

Her expertise has been featured across TV, radio, podcasts, magazines, newspapers, and global summits. Fluent in English, French, and conversational Spanish, Julie's passion for travel, meaningful connection, and authentic storytelling shines through her charismatic personality. This dynamic energy, combined with her ability to engage and inspire, has made her a popular choice for audiences and clients worldwide.

Through her books, signature events, coaching programs, and powerful keynotes, Julie has helped thousands worldwide move from fear to bold action, and from self-doubt to unstoppable momentum.

Whether speaking to a room full of executives, coaching one-on-one, or inspiring audiences around the world, her mission remains simple yet profound: to awaken greatness, nurture leadership, and remind us all that the life we dream of is already within reach.

Website: www.julieblouin.com
Email: julie@julieblouin.com

Mat Bankes

Mat Bankes is not your typical leadership speaker. He's a truth-teller, mirror-holder, and guide for those ready to remember who they are beneath the noise.

Born from his own journey through profound personal breakdown, Mat's work is rooted in the raw, lived experience of dismantling false identities and emerging with clarity, presence, and emotional integrity. His mission is not to "fix" people or organizations, but to help them remember the intelligence, connection, and courage already inside them.

With a style that blends grounded humor, deep compassion, and sharp insight, Mat supports leaders, teams, and individuals to shed performance-based leadership and step into relational, truth-based leadership. His keynotes, workshops, and culture programs ripple far beyond inspiration; they create actual shifts in self-awareness, communication, and collective trust.

Mat's work speaks to those who crave more than surface-level solutions; it calls to those ready to evolve, both personally and professionally. His contribution to this collaborative book captures the heart of his philosophy: transformation is not about adding more. It's about removing what was never true.

On stage and off, Mat embodies what he teaches: presence, clarity, and the unwavering belief that the most powerful leadership starts from within.

Mat would love to connect with you to hear what value you took away from this book.

You can connect with Mat on:
Facebook | Instagram | X (Twitter) | Linked In
@ Mat Bankes

Or if you'd like to explore working with Mat or booking him as a speaker for your next event, you can connect with Mat at:
MatBankes.com.au

Kandi Rohemhildt

Kandi is a vibrant, soulful woman who has turned life's challenges into opportunities for growth. She overcame childhood sexual abuse, divorce, and a 15-year battle with an eating disorder to become a guiding light for others seeking healing, self-discovery, and self-esteem. Her journey is a testament to resilience, self-love, and the power of the mind-body connection.

Through yoga, meditation, breathwork, and journaling, Kandi rebuilt her sense of self, realizing that confidence and self-esteem aren't found, they're remembered. She embraced conscious living, proving that true beauty radiates from within. Now in her 60s, she embodies freedom and empowerment, showing others that aging is not a limitation but a doorway to deeper self-awareness and vitality. Whether Kandi's lifting weights, kayaking in Florida's springs, or walking Gulf beaches, she lives with adventure, wellness, and purpose.

She is passionate about guiding others through transformation, helping them break free from limiting beliefs and step into their power with confidence. With her engagement at Redesign Trainings (@redesigntrainings.org), she seamlessly blends creativity about life with being in service, inspiring change with beauty and intention.

Kandi knows healing isn't a final destination. It's a lifelong journey of love, joy, self-discovery, and self-worth. With unwavering belief in transformation, she empowers others to embrace their self-esteem and live their most radiant, fulfilling lives.

Magali Dorffner

Magali Dorffner is a certified Life Coach and WILDFIT Coach, and a passionate advocate for self-discovery and personal growth. She supports women in midlife in stepping beyond limitations and creating the life they truly desire, knowing that, as Peter Drucker said, *"The best way to predict your future is to create it."*

With a background in accounting and consulting, Magali spent over a decade helping businesses thrive. Through her own self-exploration, she discovered what truly fueled her soul: supporting women in midlife as they navigate overwhelm, shifting identity, and self-doubt.

Her journey from high performance to burnout, through depression, grief, and a lack of self-care, taught her the importance of self-awareness, resilience, and the quiet power of self-esteem as a foundation for life.

As a WILDFIT Coach, Magali understands the deep connection between physical health and mental well-being. She integrates mindset and emotional awareness into her holistic wellness coaching, helping women improve their health, increase their energy, and gain clarity and confidence.

With her raw, natural ability to connect, Magali offers space for deep reflection. Women feel safe to be open and vulnerable, allowing them to grow into grounded, authentic versions of themselves.

When she's not coaching, Magali finds joy in meaningful connections, staying active, and spending time in nature with her beloved border collie, Bowie. She is always seeking the next adventure, both within and beyond.

Connect with Magali at magali@mbcd.net.au or facebook.com/magali.dorffner

Kia Stewart

Kia Stewart is a devoted mother, spiritual mentor, and sophomore at Grand Canyon University, where she is pursuing a degree in Psychology. With a lifelong passion for writing and a deep curiosity about the human mind, Kia is dedicated to understanding what drives our thoughts, behaviors, and emotional well-being.

In addition to her academic journey, Kia has completed several workshops focused on mindfulness, presence, and the art of holding space for others navigating their own spiritual paths. Her work reflects a commitment to inner growth and compassionate guidance.

This marks her second contribution to the *A Journey of Riches* series, where she continues to share her personal experiences and insights. Kia openly explores both her past and present, grounded in the belief that a happy ending is always possible, for herself and for anyone open to receiving it.

Connect with Kia

Facebook: Ladii.Kia21
Other platforms: linktr.ee/herbalangel777

Manuela Lipp

Manuela Lipp, is a transformative executive and leadership coach, passionate about guiding leaders back to their inner truth. Originally trained as a lawyer with years of corporate experience, she left a successful legal career to follow her deeper calling: to serve humanity by raising consciousness and empowering people to live and lead from within.

Her background includes systemic solution-focused coaching, life coaching, the Three Principles (*Mind, Consciousness, and Thought* by Sydney Banks), the Leadership Circle Profile™ (LCP), holistic business development, systemic consulting, and supervision. She brings a powerful blend of structure and soul to her work. Her approach is rooted in presence, deep listening, and the belief that true leadership starts with self-leadership.

Manuela's own journey, from high achiever to heart-driven coach, mirrors the path she now facilitates for others. She draws from a rich toolbox and integrates her diverse methods in a deeply intuitive and service-oriented way, always attuned to the uniqueness of the individual or organization she serves. She has a gift for sensing subtle dynamics, recognizing unspoken truths, and guiding transformation with clarity and compassion.

She serves those who are ready to grow, awaken, and embrace their true being and unfold their full potential. Manuela lives in Switzerland and is dedicated to creating spaces of clarity, connection, and transformation.

manuela.lipp@coachrgroup.ch
https://coachrgroup.ch
https://www.linkedin.com/in/manuela-lipp-9179489/

Phil Barlow

Phil Barlow is a dynamic artist, music healer, and author whose work inspires transformation and inner growth. With a voice that speaks to the soul, and words that resonate deeply, Phil channels his life experiences into music and writing that heal, empower, and uplift.

An established singer-songwriter and performer, Phil has toured nationally with hundreds of shows, playing major festivals like Woodford Folk Festival, Blues on Broadbeach, and Caloundra Music Festival, as well as sold-out house concerts and healing events. His albums, *The Awakening*, *Break Free*, and *True Evolution*, blend conscious roots and earthy blues rock, connecting with those on the path of self-discovery and inner freedom.

Phil is the author of *The Poetry of Healing: Pain to Peace* and the creator of *Peace Mind Music*, a music healing and meditation app designed to support emotional well-being.

Whether through song, performance, or writing, Phil creates heartfelt and inspiring spaces for authenticity, connection, and transformation.

Learn more at: www.philbarlowmusic.com

Leigh Huxley

Leigh was born and raised in South Africa and moved to the UK in 2000.

Now, in her wise woman years, she started her career in the beauty industry, where she owned a skincare business in Durban, South Africa, for thirteen and a half years.

She became qualified as a Spiritual Life Coach in 2020. Leigh says that looking back, she can see that she's been on a journey of "learning to love and value herself" her whole life without realizing it and says that turning 50 was the catalyst that initiated her journey of self-discovery, healing, and transformation.

She's navigated many storms, many of her own doing but some a bolt out of the blue, using the mantra: "This too shall pass; nature never makes a storm that lasts," especially when the skies were dark and the winds of emotion high.

It was, however, the aftermath of destruction and devastation that led her on a journey through the shadows of shame, guilt, infertility, infidelity, divorce, blended families, and perhaps the most challenging one, as a mom supporting her son through two psychotic episodes in the space of five years as a teenager and young adult.

Leigh discovered that kindness, compassion, and acceptance were the balms that soothed her wounds; but it was self-forgiveness that healed them. She says that her wounds are now scars that are part of the landscape of who she is, reminding her of how far she's come.

Leigh wants you to remember, "You're not alone, and you don't have to do it alone."

Contact:

Email: heavenleigh.spiritualcoaching@gmail.com
Website: www.leighhuxley.com

Piera Maria Fromm

Piera Maria Fromm came into this world with a love for movement and stillness. Her intuition and metaphysical perception have been present and encouraged from the day she was born.

She has dedicated the last fifteen-plus years to the field of mind, body, and spirit wellness. Piera is a Consciousness teacher with a wealth of experience and qualifications.

She holds diplomas in various yoga practices, meditation, Reiki, and mindfulness, to mention a few. She is also the host of the YouTube channel Piera Maria Conscious Living and offers one-on-one mentorships and courses on her website.

Piera advocates helping people integrate the practical tools she has gained over the last decade into their daily lives to bring the nervous system back to homeostasis and release stress.

For the last three years, she has been working on her book, which will be published in early 2026 and will encompass all the above principles.

Piera's life mission is to remain aligned, grounded, and connected, radiating her light in this world and touching as many hearts as possible along her journey.

Contacts

https://pieramaria.com/
https://www.youtube.com/@PieraMariaConsciousLiving
https://www.facebook.com/piera.fromm
https://www.instagram.com/pieramaria_consciousliving/

Lisa Duckworth

If you're ready to start your own transformation journey, I'm here to support you every step of the way. Whether you want to boost your health, rebuild your confidence, or live fully aligned with your purpose, together we'll unlock your inner potential and create a life filled with vitality, passion, and true fulfillment.

As a certified nutrition and fitness coach and founder of LuMarie Wellness, I also offer a Freedom Blueprint designed especially for full-time parents and anyone seeking extra income or more freedom in their life. You can explore it at dailywealthrise.com.

Connect with me on Facebook and Instagram at Lisa Duckworth, where you'll find my Beacons store packed with wellness blueprints to help you thrive: beacons.ai/lumarielifestyle.

Plus, visit my Etsy store for exclusive digital wellness tools and products: lumariewellnessstore.etsy.com, and check out my fitness journals available on Amazon:

Women's Fitness Journal
Men's Fitness Journal

Let's make your wellness and freedom goals a reality!

Liz Pembroke

In her sixties, Liz has had a rich and varied career spanning the corporate world, property development, and her own private therapeutic practice. Liz brings a broad and transformational perspective to her work. Starting as a PA, Liz later became a director in her family run property development business whilst building her own successful property venture. Alongside this, she retrained as a counsellor, dedicating many years to supporting leaders in cultivating emotional resilience and wellbeing.

For over 30 years, Liz has immersed herself in the study of human development and personal growth, training with world renowned teachers in areas such as breathwork, energy healing, mindfulness, wholefood nutrition, spirituality, theology, and emotional intelligence, not only for her clients but as part of her own lifelong journey of healing and self-discovery. Her decade-long work in prisons, delivering restorative justice and wellbeing programs, offered profound insight into the healing power of empathy and connection.

A passionate advocate for social impact, she also co-led Street Angels, supporting vulnerable individuals, and lead retreats for leaders that offered space for deep reflection and renewal.

Certified as a Transformation Life Coach with one of the UK's leading coaching bodies (ICF and AC accredited), Liz speaks from both professional expertise and lived experience when giving talks to inspire others. She is a proud mum to two grown daughters and a supportive step-mum. Liz's life journey through divorce, burnout, grief, and self-doubt, has equipped her to be a life-changing coach, speaker, and guide for others.

Matthew White

Matthew White is a visionary coach, entrepreneur, and author dedicated to helping coaches and consultants transform their passion into thriving businesses. With a clear, authentic voice and a heart-centered approach, he shares wisdom and practical strategies that empower others to build impactful, scalable coaching practices.

As the founder of Coach Launch, Matthew has supported thousands of coaches worldwide in breaking through barriers and creating sustainable success. His work is rooted in a deep understanding of the coaching industry combined with real-world business experience, offering guidance that is both inspiring and actionable.

Matthew's mission is to create a ripple effect of transformation by equipping coaches with the tools, mindset, and confidence to serve their clients fully while growing their own freedom and fulfillment.

Whether through coaching programs, workshops, or his writing, Matthew cultivates spaces of growth, clarity, and empowerment for coaches ready to make a difference.

Learn more at: coachlaunch.com

Rebecca Sarr

Rebecca Sarr is the founder of Quantum Empathy Technique (QET), a profound healing and awakening method based on the principles of empathic resonance. A former human rights lawyer, with a PhD in the Anthropology of Consciousness, she developed QET through more than a decade of theoretical research and spiritual practice.

Rebecca's expertise focuses on embodiment and intercorporeality, the spirituality of music and rhythm, energetics and healing, channeling and extrasensory experience, and human potential and spiritually-based transformation.

She offers groundbreaking QET programs that support people to activate their empathic genius, connect with their soul's purpose, and live powerfully from the heart space.

Through the Quantum Mastery Academy (QMA), Rebecca also offers QET Practitioner training courses, guiding students to shift from empathic overwhelm to quantum mastery, share their gifts with the world, and realize their potential as the leaders of the future.

If you'd like to learn more about becoming a Quantum Empath, joining a QMA program, or enrolling in QET practitioner training, visit www.rebeccasarr.com.

John R Spender

John Spender is a 43-time international best-selling co-author, who didn't learn how to read and write at a basic level until he was ten years old. He has since traveled to 75 different countries and territories and started many businesses leading him to create the best-selling book series *A Journey of Riches*. He is an award-winning international speaker and movie maker.

John worked as an international NLP trainer and has coached thousands of people from various backgrounds through all sorts of challenges. From the borderline homeless to very wealthy individuals, he has helped many people to get in touch with their truth to create a life on their terms.

John's search for answers to living a fulfilling life has taken him to work with Native American Indians in the hills of San Diego, the forests of Madagascar, swimming with humpback whales in Tonga, exploring the Okavango Delta of Botswana, and the Great Wall of China. He's traveled from Chile to Slovakia, Hungary to the Solomon Islands, the mountains of Italy, and the streets of Mexico. Everywhere his journey has taken him, John has discovered a hunger among people to find a new way to live, with a yearning for freedom of expression. His belief that everyone has a book in them was born.

He is now a writing coach, having worked with more than 400 authors from 50 different countries for the *A Journey of Riches* series http://ajourneyofriches.com/ and his publishing house, Motion Media International, has published 58 non-fiction titles to date.

John also wrote and produced the movie documentary *The Gift in Adversity* starring Jack Canfield, Rev. Michael Bernard Beckwith, and Dr. John Demartini. The trailer was just launched on YouTube: https://youtu.be/e7IIBHZ8lCQ.

"Self-esteem is as important to our well-being as legs are to a table. It is essential for physical and mental health and for happiness."

— Louise Hart

AFTERWORD

I hope you enjoyed the heartfelt stories, wisdom, and vulnerability shared in this book. Storytelling is the oldest form of communication, and I hope you feel inspired to take a step toward living a fulfilling life. Feel free to contact any of the authors in this book or the other books in this series.

The proceeds of this book will be used for social giving at Jewel Children's Home in Northeast Bali.

Other books in the series are...

Building Self-Confidence: *A Journey of Riches*, Book Forty
https://www.amazon.com/dp/B0F5PWWHPG

Unlock Your Hidden Potential: *A Journey of Riches*, Book Thirty-Nine
https://www.amazon.com/dp/B0DXVKT6KH

Follow Your Soul's Calling: A Journey of Riches, Book Thirty-Eight
https://www.amazon.com/dp/B0DQJYLBHY

The Power of Self-Discovery: A Journey of Riches, Book Thirty-Seven
https://www.amazon.com/dp/B0D4K35JFP

Elevating Your Life: A Journey of Riches, Book Thirty-Six
https://www.amazon.com/dp/B0CZWRJ94Y

Afterword

Living the Paradigm of Kindness: A Journey of Riches, Book Thirty-Five
https://www.amazon.com/dp/B0CSXF1FBV

Creating Resilience: A Journey of Riches, Book Thirty-Four
https://www.amazon.com/dp/B0CNVRDY38

Discover Your Purpose: A Journey of Riches, Book Thirty-Three
https://www.amazon.com/dp/B0CFDLWTCB

Live Your Passion: A Journey of Riches, Book Thirty-Two
https://www.amazon.com/Live-Your-Passion-Stories-Fulfilling-ebook/dp/B0C5QXMNRQ

Master Your Mindset: A Journey of Riches, Book Thirty-One
https://mybook.to/MasterYourMindset

Transform Your Wounds into Wisdom: A Journey of Riches, Book Thirty
https://www.amazon.com/dp/ B0BKTJ377N

Motivate Your Life: A Journey of Riches, Book Twenty-Nine
https://www.amazon.com/dp/B0BCXMF11P

Awaken to Your Inner Truth: A Journey of Riches, Book Twenty-Eight
https://www.amazon.com/dp/B09YLYMQ4H?geniuslink=true

The Power of Inspiration: A Journey of Riches, Book Twenty-Seven
http://mybook.to/ThePowerofInspiration

Messages from The Heart: A Journey of Riches, Book Twenty-Six
http://mybook.to/MessagesOfHeart

Abundant Living: A Journey of Riches, Book Twenty-Five
https://www.amazon.com/dp/B0963N6B2C

The Way of the Leader: A Journey of Riches, Book Twenty-Four
https://www.amazon.com/dp/1925919285

The Attitude of Gratitude: *A Journey of Riches,* Book Twenty-Three
https://www.amazon.com/dp/1925919269

Facing Your Fears: *A Journey of Riches,* Book Twenty-Two
https://www.amazon.com/dp/1925919218

Returning to Love: *A Journey of Riches,* Book Twenty-One
https://www.amazon.com/dp/B08C54M2RB

Develop Inner Strength: *A Journey of Riches,* Book Twenty
https://www.amazon.com/dp/1925919153

Building your Dreams: A Journey of Riches, Book Nineteen
https://www.amazon.com/dp/B081KZCN5R

Liberate your Struggles: A Journey of Riches, Book Eighteen
https://www.amazon.com/dp/1925919099

In Search of Happiness: A Journey of Riches, Book Seventeen
https://www.amazon.com/dp/B07R8HMP3K

Tapping into Courage: A Journey of Riches, Book Sixteen
https://www.amazon.com/dp/B07NDCY1KY

The Power Healing: A Journey of Riches, Book Fifteen
https://www.amazon.com/dp/B07LGRJQ2S

The Way of the Entrepreneur: A Journey of Riches, Book Fourteen
https://www.amazon.com/dp/B07KNHYR8V

Discovering Love and Gratitude: A Journey of Riches, Book Thirteen
https://www.amazon.com/dp/B07H23Q6D1

Transformational Change: A Journey of Riches, Book Twelve
https://www.amazon.com/dp/B07FYHMQRS

Finding Inspiration: A Journey of Riches, Book Eleven
https://www.amazon.com/dp/B07F1LS1ZW

Building your Life from Rock Bottom: A Journey of Riches, Book Ten
https://www.amazon.com/dp/B07CZK155Z

Transformation Calling: A Journey of Riches, Book Nine
https://www.amazon.com/dp/B07BWQY9FB

Letting Go and Embracing the New: A Journey of Riches, Book Eight
https://www.amazon.com/dp/B079ZKT2C2

Making Empowering Choices: A Journey of Riches, Book Seven
https://www.amazon.com/Making-Empowering-Choices-Journey-Riches-ebook/dp/B078JXMK5V

The Benefit of Challenge: A Journey of Riches, Book Six
https://www.amazon.com/dp/B0778S2VBD

Personal Changes: A Journey of Riches, Book Five
https://www.amazon.com/dp/B075WCQM4N

Dealing with Changes in Life: A Journey of Riches, Book Four
https://www.amazon.com/dp/B0716RDKK7

Making Changes: A Journey of Riches, Book Three
https://www.amazon.com/dp/B01MYWNI5A

The Gift in Challenge: A Journey of Riches, Book Two
https://www.amazon.com/dp/B01GBEML4G

From Darkness into the Light: A Journey of Riches, Book One
https://www.amazon.com/dp/B018QMPHJW

Thank you to all the authors who have shared aspects of their lives in hopes of inspiring others to live a bigger, fuller version of themselves.

I want to share a beautiful quote from Jim Rohn: "You can't complain and feel grateful at the same time." At any given moment, we can either feel like a victim of life or be connected and grateful for it. I hope this book helps you feel grateful and inspires you to pursue your dreams.

For more information about contributing to the series, visit our website: http://ajourneyofriches.com/. Furthermore, if you enjoyed reading this book, we would appreciate your review on Amazon to help get our message out to even more readers.